AMERICANA

QUILTS

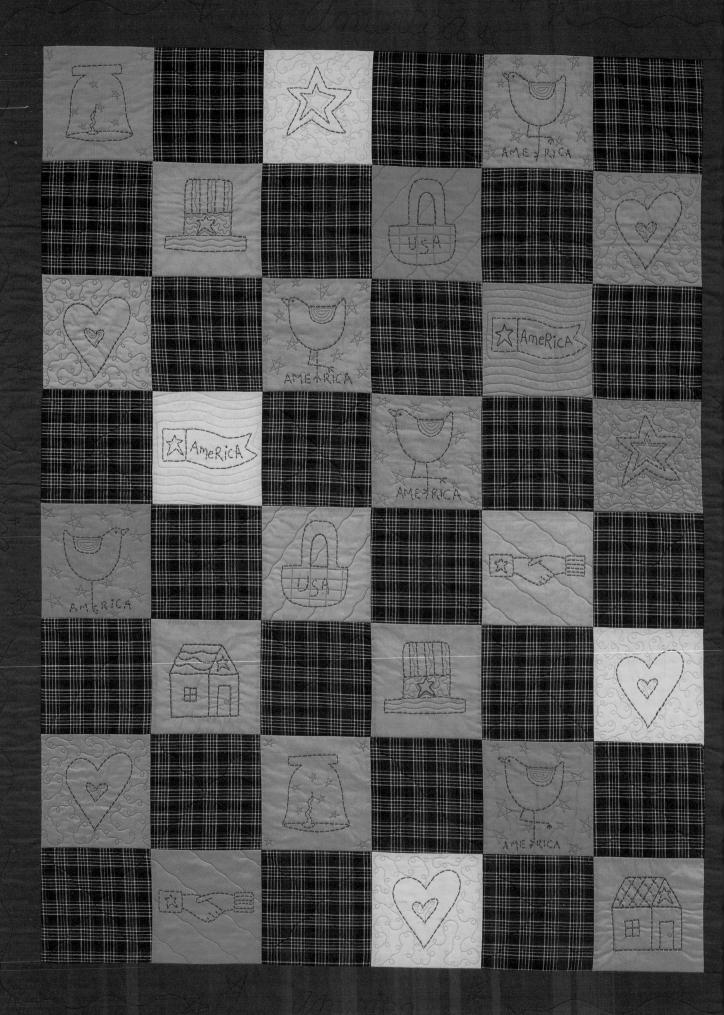

AMERICANA QUILTS

SANDY BONSIB

Martingale™
& COMPANY

Americana Quilts
© 2003 by Sandy Bonsib

Martingale & Company
20205 144th Avenue NE
Woodinville, WA 98072-8478
www.martingale-pub.com

Printed in China
08 07 06 05 04 03   8 7 6 5 4 3 2 1

Library of Congress Cataloging-in-Publication Data
Bonsib, Sandy
   Americana quilts / Sandy Bonsib.
      p. cm.
   ISBN 1-56477-465-1
   1. Patchwork–Patterns. 2. Quilting–Patterns.
   3. Americana in art. I. Title.
   TT835 .B6276 2003
   746.46'041–dc21
                                              2002153995

MISSION STATEMENT

We are dedicated to providing quality products and service by working together to inspire creativity and to enrich the lives we touch.

CREDITS

President ❖ Nancy J. Martin
CEO ❖ Daniel J. Martin
Publisher ❖ Jane Hamada
Editorial Director ❖ Mary V. Green
Managing Editor ❖ Tina Cook
Technical Editor ❖ Dawn Anderson
Copy Editor ❖ Liz McGehee
Design Director ❖ Stan Green
Illustrator ❖ Laurel Strand
Cover Designer ❖ Stan Green
Text Designer ❖ Regina Girard
Photographer ❖ Brent Kane

This book is dedicated to two very special men in my life:

To my stepdad, Carl Brandt.

Almost twenty years ago, my mom married Carl, and he immediately embraced us, her three daughters, as his own. Thank you, Dad, for being such an important part of my life, for loving my mother so much, for loving me like a daughter, and for being my children's beloved Grampy. You are so kind and so giving. We are all lucky you came into our lives.

To my uncle, Richard Bonsib.

Uncle Dick has always been an important part of my life. Many years ago, when I was ten or eleven years old, I suggested that because "she is so pretty," he should marry the wonderful lady who has become my Aunt Gretchen. I babysat for their two children when they were little, watched them grow up, and now admire pictures of Dick and Gretchen's grandchildren.

Thank you, Uncle Dick, for being a wonderful uncle, always warm, often laughing. You have always been so proud of your family—all of us, your nieces and nephews, as well as your own children—as we have grown up and become the people we are today. And now your courage and determination as you live with Parkinson's disease is awesome and inspiring.

I love you both very much.

Acknowledgments

Without the help of my husband, John Bickley, and my children, Ben and Kate, I would never be able to write books. They help me with endless details as I work, and they take over many daily chores so I can meet my deadlines. You are the best!

Additional thanks go to:

Sue Van Gerpen, for sharing her charming and extensive collection of Americana objects. Her generosity in lending this collection to me for use in this book is greatly appreciated. Thank you, Sue, for making this book so much better.

Becky Kraus, my machine quilter for many years. I continue to appreciate her wonderfully creative ideas and beautiful workmanship.

Kathy Staley, who machine quilted two quilts in this book. She is just beginning her machine quilting career, but her creativity and excellent work add so much to my quilts.

My many students around the country who have taken my classes and made wonderful quilts. I continue to learn as much from you as you have learned from me.

Dawn Anderson, my editor. It has been a pleasure to work with you. Thank you for all that you have done to make this book the best that it can be.

Finally, thank you to Martingale & Company, for once again believing in me.

Contents

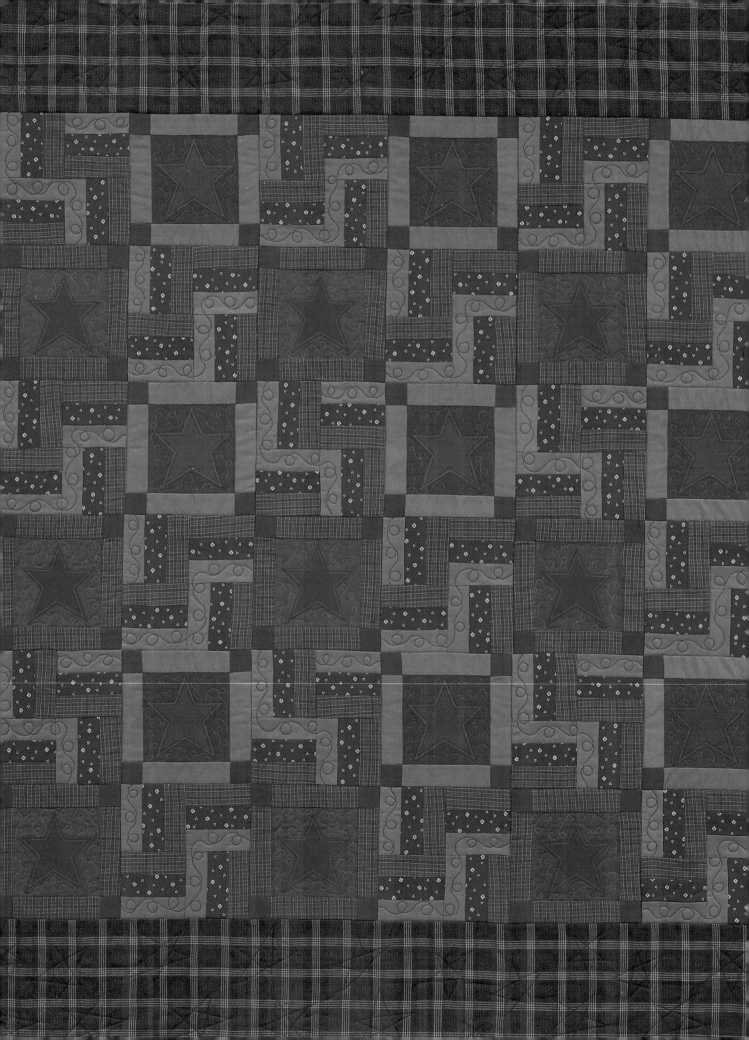

Preface

"America the Beautiful."

These words took on new meaning for me after September 11, 2001. After that day, I found myself looking for Americana items everywhere. I wanted to have them, display them, just look at them. I hadn't yet thought of creating them myself.

Never have I seen a country so diverse come together so united as I have since that date. I felt that writing this book and making these quilts would be a way to cope with my feelings of loss, helplessness, and sadness—especially sadness—after that tragic day. I have never made quilts as a response to grief; I have always made quilts just because I loved making them. But as I made quilt after quilt for this book, I discovered that I was able to work through the sadness and enjoy making the quilts as an expression of my pride and my patriotism.

I discovered that I have two types of tears for September 11. My first tears are for all of the families and friends who lost their loved ones and for all of America. But I also have tears of pride when I look around and see our flag flying proud, the many heroes that aided and are still aiding those in need, and the way we have all united.

Enjoy these quilt projects. Make them, change them, play with them, and display them with pride. Americana quilts truly are a celebration of our patriotism and our pride. These quilts are not just for the Fourth of July, but for all year and for any time.

My Name Is Old Glory

I am the flag of the United States of America.
My name is Old Glory.
I fly atop the world's tallest buildings.
I stand watch in America's halls of justice.
I fly majestically over institutions of learning.
I stand guard with the greatest military power
in the world.
Look up! And see me.

Howard Schnauber

What Is Americana?

There is more than one way to define Americana. When I considered titles for this book, the title and subtitle that originally came to mind were "Americana Quilts: The Heart of Folk Art." In a sense, everything created by an American folk artist is a piece of Americana. By this definition, then, Americana would include a wide variety of objects, such as trade signs, carvings, decoys, scrimshaw, carousel animals, weathervanes and whirligigs, baskets, ceramics, dolls and dollhouses, paintings, tinware, toys, and furniture, as well as textiles such as quilts, woven coverlets, cross-stitch and needlepoint, and rag rugs.

Who created American folk art? Untrained artists. Folk artists, as compared to fine artists, were unschooled in their art. Folk artists weren't professionals. Their work had imperfections, missing details, and often awkward proportions. The artists didn't know how to make a piece "right." Folk art was made by hand, usually to fulfill a need, and these objects were constructed using materials at hand. If the artist ran out of something, he or she substituted something else. Folk art objects, although one of a kind, were everyday articles expected to be

used and used up. They were not considered valuable. Thus, few folk artists, including our quiltmaking grandmothers, signed their work.

Where did American folk art come from? In its pure form, it came from wherever the people who created it came from. Newcomers brought folk art from their home countries, carrying on the traditions they knew and going further, exploring new ideas and working with new materials found in their adopted land.

Learning to work with new materials was required because the materials used in immigrants' homelands were often unavailable in America. And these immigrants had a very real and often immediate need for useful objects. Most people in early America lived in rural areas, and they had limited access to ready-made products. The solution? To make things themselves. People learned to craft what they needed, using what they had on hand. Never mind that they didn't have the same kind of wood, the same colors of paint, or the

same fibers for textiles that they used before. American ingenuity was born. Thus, while the resemblance of American folk art to its historic form is often recognizable, the dictates of time and materials gradually modified many folk art forms into a new style, sometimes a style hardly resembling the original.

Objects were handed down within families, repaired again and again, and kept in use until they were truly beyond repair. Everything was made to last as long as possible, with any added decoration giving pleasure to the user. Weddings and births were commemorated in embroideries and paintings, portraits of family pets were hooked into rugs, and biblical characters were stitched into quilts. Objects such as these, and more, became the essence of a remarkable body of work we call folk art.

Certain communities retained their folk art traditions in a purer form than others. The Shakers, as well as the Amish and the Mennonites, formed strong communities in America, and their folk art for many years remained largely unchanged, modified only by the materials available. There wasn't much blending and melding into an American form in these communities.

In 1776 Americans made a formal decision to form a new country and be free. From that time onward, our folk art added a political dimension and took on a new direction. This is the second definition of Americana—not just folk art made in America, but also America-themed objects in particular. Certain subjects became symbols of freedom— Lady Liberty, the eagle, and the United States flag. Lady Liberty symbolizes the freedom that the United States Constitution promised to all citizens. She was given a specific, fixed form when the Statue of Liberty was erected in 1886, standing at the entrance to New York's harbor. The bald eagle was approved by Congress as the national emblem of the United States on June 20, 1782. And the American flag, with its red and white stripes and white stars on a blue background, seemed adaptable to many forms.

"Politicians and merchants, quick to capitalize on the cult of the flag, appropriated the popular icon for their own purposes. Politicians printed their campaign slogans and portraits on flag banners, and merchants unabashedly wrapped their wares in flag packaging and made the Stars and Stripes part of their trademark. By the late 1890s, the Stars and Stripes could be seen on everything from pincushions and pillowcases to clown costumes and pickled pork. In the absence of official flag guidelines, flag makers, commercial enterprises, and private citizens were free to follow their own fancy—and did."

Gerald C. Wertkin

From *Long May She Wave: A Graphic History of the American Flag* by Kit Hinrichs and Delphine Hirasuna

One of the most widely recognized Americana motifs, the flag is symbolic all by itself. Interestingly enough, the Continental Congress left no record to show why it chose red, white, and blue as the colors for the flag. In fact, our original flag was used for very practical reasons: fighting for independence, our colonies needed a way to identify their naval ships.

The blue field behind the stars stands for vigilance, perseverance, and justice. The resolution passed by Congress in 1777 stated that the flag should have thirteen stars, one for each state in the Union. But Congress didn't indicate how the stars should be arranged. Throughout our history, the stars have therefore appeared in many ways—in rows, sometimes even and sometimes staggered, in a circle, in a larger star pattern, in geometric shapes, and in random order. Early stars were five-pointed, six-pointed, even seven-pointed and eight-pointed, depending on the maker.

The stripes in the flag stand for the thirteen original colonies. The white stripes reflect purity and innocence. The red stripes symbolize valor and courage.

Congress originally intended to increase the flag by one star and one stripe every time a new state was added to the union. By 1794, two new states had joined the original thirteen, thus a fifteen-stripe flag was used after May 1, 1795 and was displayed until the War of 1812. It was this flag that inspired Francis Scott Key to write the poem destined to become *The Star-Spangled Banner*. Then, by 1817, five more states had entered the Union. Congress could quickly see that with other territories applying to be states, our flag's wide stripes could quickly be reduced to pinstripes. It was proposed that the flag revert to its original thirteen stripes, adding only a new star to the flag on the next July 4th after each state joined the Union.

Since new states were frequently added, twenty-eight alone between 1818 and 1912, the American flag was always changing. At times in our history, practical flag makers left gaps in the field so that new stars could be stitched into place.

The flag that was in use the longest to date was the forty eight–star flag, flown for forty-seven years, from 1912 until 1959, when Alaska joined the Union.

A 13-Star Design, 1777

A 15-Star Design, 1795

A 26-Star Design, 1837

A 27-Star Design, 1845

A 33-Star Design, 1859

A 37-Star Design, 1867

13

The flag, originally a military symbol, became a revered national symbol during the Civil War. At that time, the flag came to be seen as a symbol of preserving the Union. At times the Star-Spangled Banner was raised in every town and village north of the Mason-Dixon Line. Reverence intensified when the flag accompanied soldiers going off to battle and when it was draped over coffins. Enthusiasm for displaying the flag increased again with the celebration of America's centennial in 1876. It wasn't until 1892 that flags were raised on all schoolhouses. That same year, The Pledge of Allegiance was written, although Congress did not officially recognize the pledge until 1942.

This enthusiasm, accompanied by a lack of official rules about how our flag should and shouldn't be used, yielded a wealth of creative interpretations of our flag. Thus flag objects have become more than a unique part of our heritage. They have created their own genre of folk art.

America is not like a blanket—one piece of unbroken cloth, the same texture, the same size. America is more like a quilt—many patches, many pieces, many colors, many sizes, all wove and held together by a common thread.

Henry M. Jackson

14

Folk Colors and Fabric Choices

We associate certain colors with folk art. Originally, these colors came from natural sources. The roots of the madder plant made a deep red, boiled walnuts produced a rich, dark brown, boiled chestnuts created a buff brown, powdered brick dust and baked yellow clay both made a reddish brown, flowers and clay made differing shades of yellow, and soot produced black.

Add the effects of age to these colors, and they change—either fading or, if protected by varnish, taking on a yellowish tone, resulting in a softer, warmer appearance. Of course, if we use these "aged" colors, we're employing folk art colors as they appear now, rather than the way they would have looked when freshly made. But that's permissible. The patina and fading of age are the look we now associate with folk art.

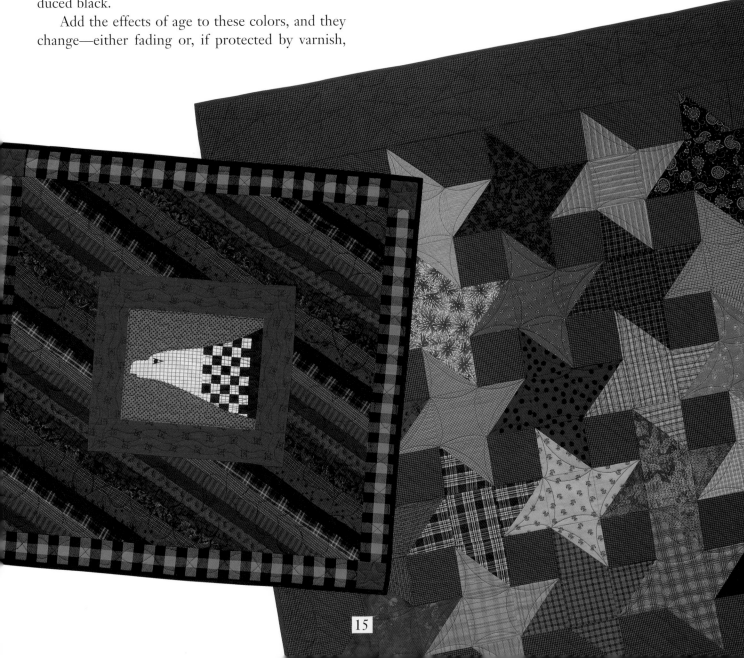

FOLK ART COLORS

Folk art colors include a variety of tints, shades, and tones. For example:

Red can be dark red, grayed pink, or red-orange.   **Green can be dark or grayed.**

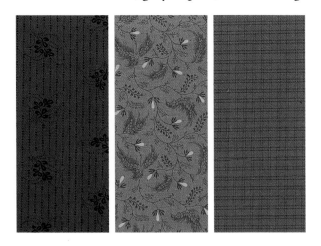   

Blue might not be just bright blue,   **Purple can be a true violet**
but also dark or grayed.   **or extend to blue-violet or red-violet.**

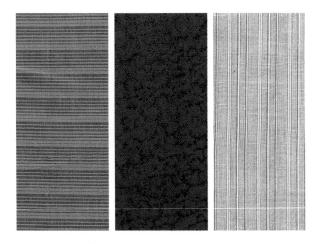   

Yellow can include pumpkin gold or mustard.   **Brown can be chocolate, tan, or cream.**

AMERICANA COLORS

For a patriotic theme, focusing on a red-white-and-blue combination can produce some wonderful, perhaps unexpectedly diverse, results.

1. Start with the basic red, white, and blue color combination.

2. Tweak it a little, making the red more mottled, the white creamier, the blue darker.

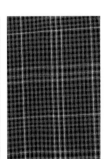

3. Or make the white tan.

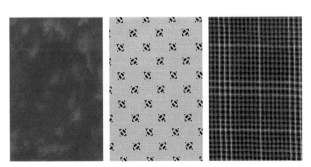

4. Add a black check to the red, substitute gold for white, and darken the blue to navy.

5. Or brighten the navy to a true blue.

6. To really stretch, the blue can become black.

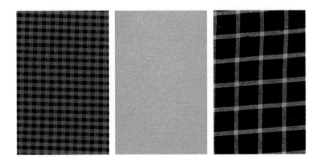

Any combination of these colors—or any combination of these combinations—could contribute to an Americana feel or a patriotic theme. Notice that Americana color combinations include a warm color (red), a cool color (blue or black), and a neutral color (white, cream, tan, or gold). One reason this color combination is so pleasing is that it reflects complementary relationships—warm vs. cool, light vs. dark—which our eyes find harmonious.

Stitch It! America

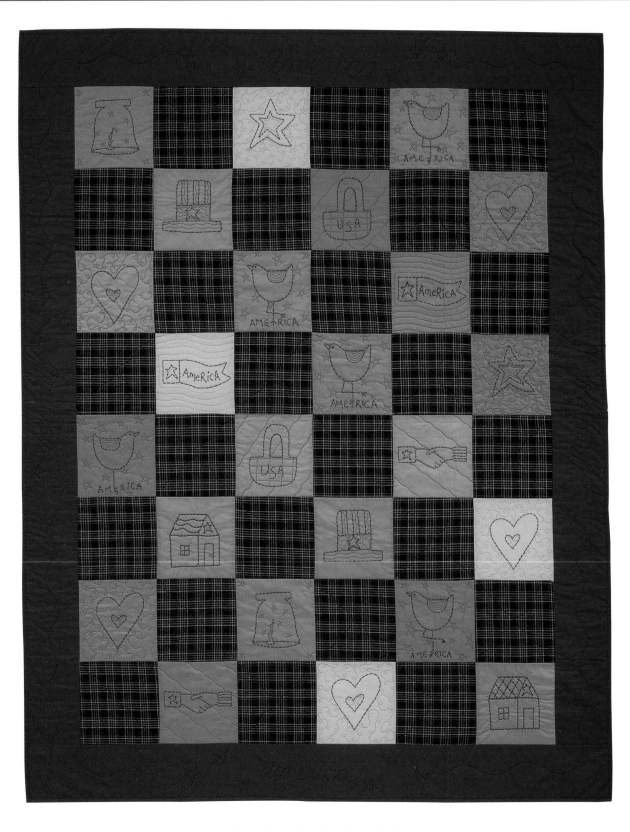

59" x 75". Quilted by Kathy Staley.

I combined my love of folk art motifs, stitching, and simple piecing to create this quilt. My daughter, Kate Bickley, helped me design these uniquely American motifs.

FABRIC	CUTTING
Yardage is based on 42"-wide fabric.	*Measurements include ¼" seam allowances.*
1¾ yds. dark blue plaid for plain blocks	24 squares, 8½" x 8½"
⅓ yd. *each* of 4 assorted gold solids and ⅝ yd. of 1 gold solid for stitched blocks	24 squares total, 8½" x 8½"
1¾ yds. dark red solid for borders and binding	7 strips, 5¾" x 42" 7 strips, 2" x 42"
4 yds. for backing (with a horizontal seam)	
63" x 79" piece of batting	
Template plastic	
Fine-line permanent marker	
2 skeins of dark blue pearl cotton, size 5	
Chenille needle, size 22	

DIRECTIONS

1. Trace the Hat, Heart, House, Bird, Hands, Bell, Star, Basket, and Flag patterns (pages 21–25) onto template plastic, using a fine-line permanent marker; cut the templates out on the drawn lines. Do not add seam allowances. Using your preferred marking tool, trace one template onto each gold square. You will need to trace two Hats, five Hearts, two Houses, five Birds, two Hands, two Bells, two Stars, two Baskets, and two Flags.

2. Using pearl cotton and a chenille needle, stitch along the marked lines, using a running stitch as on page 71. Make the stitches long and the spaces between the stitches very short, as shown on page 20, so the stitched line looks almost solid from a distance. Note that in one of my

House blocks, I changed the diamond pattern on the roof to random horizontal, wavy lines. I also reversed one of my bird designs for added interest. Make 24 stitched squares total.

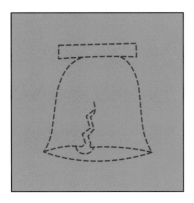

3. Arrange the stitched squares and blue plaid squares into eight rows of six blocks each, using the photo as a guide for placement. Vary the placement of the stitched blocks as desired.

4. Sew the blocks together in horizontal rows, pressing the seams in opposite directions from row to row. Sew the rows together.

5. For each side border, sew two border strips together end to end. Trim each pieced strip to 64½" long. Sew the border strips to the sides of the quilt top. Press the seams toward the border.

6. Sew the remaining border strips together end to end. Cut the pieced strip in half, and trim each half to 59" long. Sew the border strips to the top and bottom of the quilt top. Press the seams toward the border.

7. Layer the quilt top with the batting and backing; baste. Quilt as desired. Sew the binding strips together end to end. (See page 75.) Bind the edges and label your quilt.

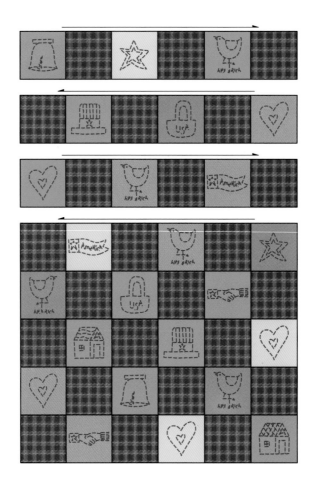

Hat

Heart

House

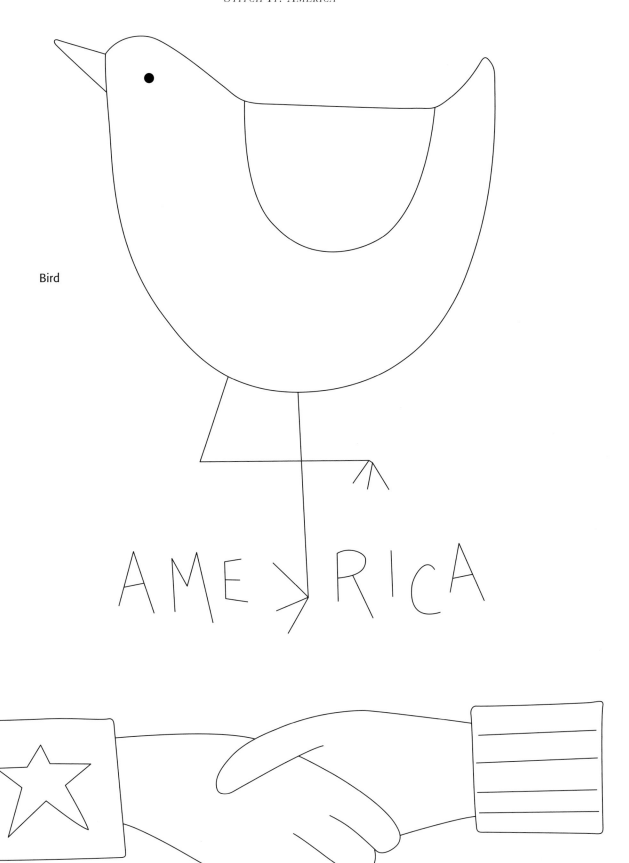

Bird

AME RICA

Hands

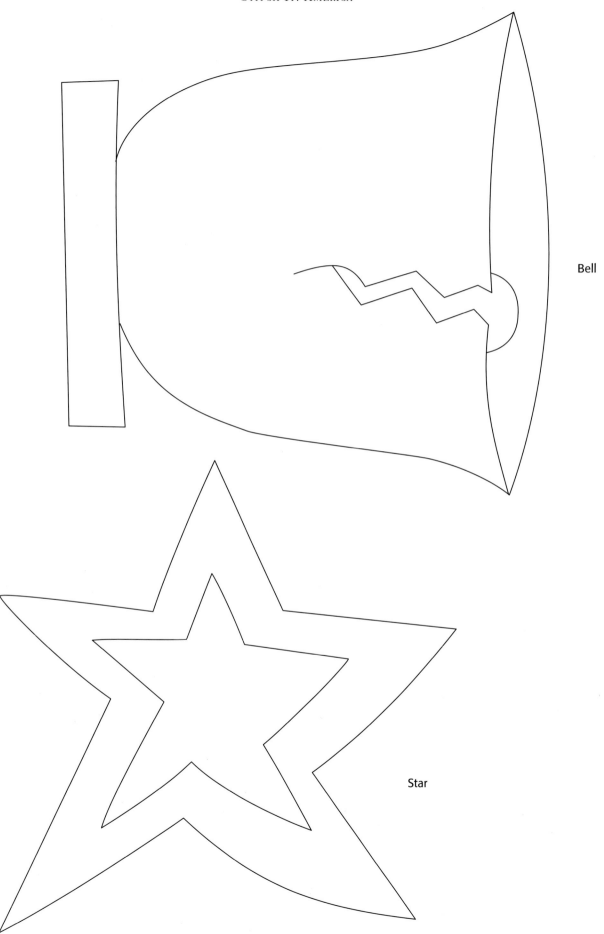

Bell

Star

Basket

Flag

What Goes Around Comes Around

42½" x 42½". Quilted by Becky Kraus.

Although I always enjoy playing with ideas and I love to make flag blocks, I had already made most of the quilts in this book when I began this one. I couldn't make another flag quilt—or could I? Maybe I could if I changed the flags so that they didn't look like those I had already made. Inspired by my collection of stars-and-stripes fabrics and by a local teacher, Reynola Pakusich, and her circular design quilts, I created my own circular flags.

FABRIC	CUTTING
Yardage is based on 42"-wide fabric.	Measurements include ¼" seam allowances.
Background Blocks	
1⅜ yds. *each* of 2 light blue fabrics**	5 squares from *each* fabric, 13½" x 13½"
Flag Blocks	

¼ yd. (or 1 fat quarter) *each* of 3 star prints	9 squares total, 6" x 6", as follows:
	    5 squares from your favorite fabric
	    2 squares from one fabric
	    2 squares from another fabric

⅝ yd. red-and-white striped fabric	5 squares, 6" x 6"* 5 rectangles, 6" x 11½"*
¼ yd. each of 2 red fabrics	1 square from each fabric, 6" x 6" 1 rectangle from each fabric, 6" x 11½"
¼ yd. blue fabric	1 square, 6" x 6" 1 rectangle, 6" x 11½"
¼ yd. blue-and-red mottled fabric	1 square, 6" x 6" 1 rectangle, 6" x 11½"
½ yd. red solid for first and third borders	2 strips, 1½" x 36½" 2 strips, 1½" x 38½" 2 strips, 1½" x 40½" 3 strips, 1½" x 42"
¼ yd. light blue fabric for second border**	2 strips, 1½" x 38½" 2 strips, 1½" x 40½"
2½ yds. for backing	
⅓ yd. light blue fabric for binding**	5 strips, 2" x 42"
47" x 47" piece of batting	
Invisible thread (optional) for machine appliqué, or thread to match flag fabrics	

*Each 6" striped square will be sewn to a 6" star square, with the resulting unit sewn to the upper long edge of a 6" x 11½" striped rectangle. Cut striped squares and rectangles so that the stripe pattern is horizontal, planning cutting carefully so that after the ¼" seam allowance is sewn, a red stripe will be next to a white stripe.

**I used only two different light blue fabrics in my quilt. If you wish to do the same, you will need 1⅜ yards of one light blue fabric for the blocks and 2 yards of a second light blue fabric for the blocks, second border, and binding.

DIRECTIONS

1. Sew a 6" square of your favorite star print to a 6" square of red-and-white stripe. Sew the pieced unit to a 6" x 11½" red-and-white striped rectangle. Repeat to make five Flag blocks total, using the same fabrics. Make four additional Flag blocks from the remaining flag fabrics.

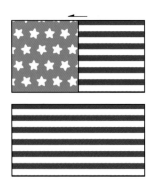

Make 9 total.

2. Using the Half-Circle pattern on page 30, make a circle template from paper. Fold the template in half, then in half again to crease. Place the template on the wrong side of the Flag block, centering the creases on the seam lines. Lightly trace around the template with a pencil or pen (a pen won't drag on the fabric). Cut out the circle ¼" beyond the traced line.

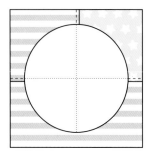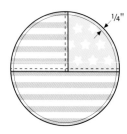

3. Sew a running stitch around the circle, inside the seam allowance. Place the template back on the wrong side of the block. Pull the thread from your running stitch to gather the fabric around the edges of the template. Press the seam allowance on the wrong side, turn over, and then press on the right side. Remove the template. You can reuse the same template to gather and press all nine flags.

Make 9.

4. To make the background blocks, pair 2 different 13½" light blue squares with right sides together. Draw a diagonal line on the wrong side of one of the fabrics. Sew ¼" from each side of the marked line. Cut on the marked line. You will have ten blocks; only nine are needed for this project.

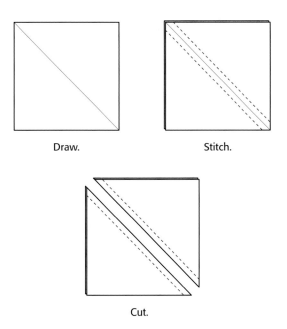

Draw.   Stitch.

Cut.

5. Press the seams to one side. Trim the blocks to 12½" x 12½". (If you have a 12½" square ruler, this is especially easy to do.)

6. Arrange the background blocks into three rows of three blocks, positioning the background fabrics as shown.

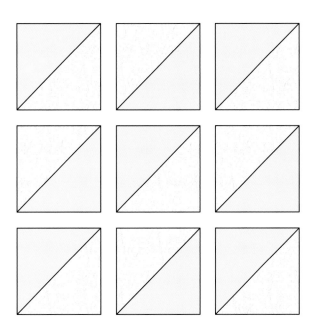

7. Center the flags on the background blocks, and pin them in place. Using your favorite appliqué method, stitch the flags to the background blocks. (I used transparent thread and a machine hem stitch.)

8. Arrange the completed blocks back into 3 rows of 3 blocks. Sew the blocks together in horizontal rows, pressing the seams in opposite directions from row to row. Sew the rows together.

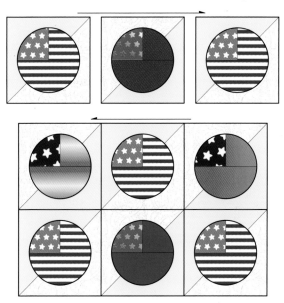

9. For the first border, sew a 1½" x 36½" red border strip to each side of the quilt top. Press the seams toward the border. Sew the 1½" x 38½" red border strips to the top and bottom of the quilt top. Press the seams toward the border.

10. For the second border, sew a 1½" x 38½" light blue border strip to each side of the quilt top. Press the seams as desired. Sew the 1½" x 40½" light blue border strips to the top and bottom of the quilt top. Press the seams as desired.

11. For the third border, sew a 1½" x 40½" red border strip to each side of the quilt top. Press the seams toward the red border. Sew the three 1½" x 42" red border strips together end to end. From that strip, cut two pieces 42½" long. Sew the strips to the top and bottom of the quilt top. Press the seams toward the red border.

12. Layer the quilt top with the batting and backing; baste. Quilt as desired. Sew the binding strips together end to end. (See page 75.) Bind the edges and label your quilt.

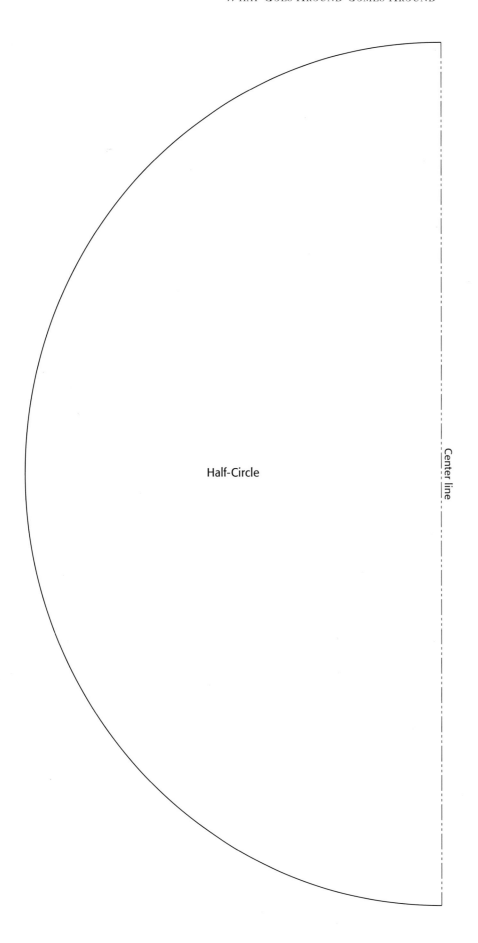

Half-Circle

Center line

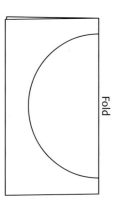

Fold

Fold a large piece of paper
in half. Place the center line
of the half-circle pattern on
the fold. Cut 1 to make circle.

Flying Proud

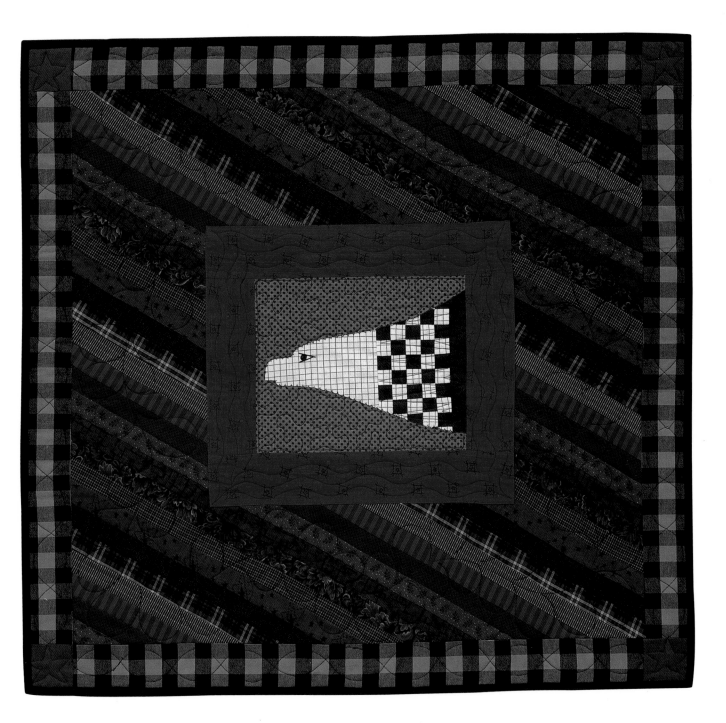

34¼" x 32½". Quilted by Becky Kraus.

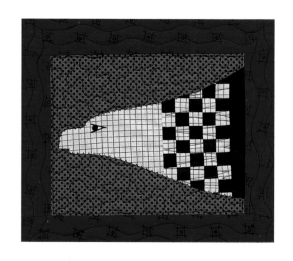

Eagle motifs have always appealed to me. I've also always found M.C. Escher's illusional drawings interesting. This quilt evolved as a result of combining these two inspirations into one piece. I especially like the diagonal background strips because they give the illusion of movement.

FABRIC	CUTTING
Yardage is based on 42"-wide fabric.	*Measurements include ¼" seam allowances.*
Eagle Block	
⅓ yd. tan print	1 rectangle, 9¼" x 11¼"
¼ yd. white print	1 rectangle, 4½" x 6½" 1 strip, 1¼" x 42"
¼ yd. dark brown print or plaid	1 rectangle, 2" x 8" 1 strip, 1¼" x 42"
¼ yd. red print	2 strips, 3" x 9¼" 2 strips, 3" x 16¼"
¼ yd. *each* of 9 assorted medium brown fabrics and 1 dark brown fabric for pieced background	4 strips *each*, 1½" x 42"
½ yd. bold black-and-tan plaid for border	2 strips, 2¾" x 28" 2 strips, 2¾" x 29¾"
⅛ yd. brown solid for corner squares	4 squares, 2¾" x 2¾"
1⅛ yds. for backing	
⅓ yd. black solid for binding	4 strips, 2" x 42"
37" x 39" piece of batting	
¼ yd. lightweight, paper-backed fusible web (optional)	
Dark brown thread for appliqué (optional)	
Black pearl cotton, size 5, and a chenille needle, size 22, or a fine-point permanent marker for making the Eagle's eye	
Red thread for appliqué (optional)	

DIRECTIONS

1. Join the 1¼" x 42" white and dark brown strips together to make a strip set. From the strip set, cut 30 segments, each 1¼" wide. Join six segments end to end. Repeat four more times to make five pieced units.

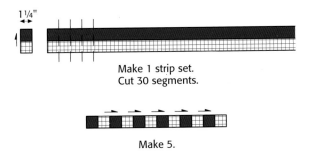

1¼"

Make 1 strip set.
Cut 30 segments.

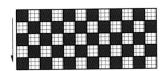

Make 5.

2. Join the pieced units together as shown to make a checkerboard unit.

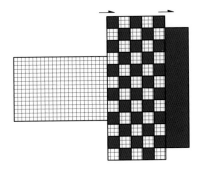

3. Join one long edge of the 2" x 8" dark brown rectangle to a long edge of the checkerboard unit, centering the rectangle along the edge of the checkerboard unit. Join 1 short edge of the 4½" x 6½" white rectangle to the opposite side of the checkerboard unit, centering the rectangle along the edge of the checkerboard unit.

4. Referring to "Fusible Appliqué" on page 70, trace the Eagle pattern (page 35) onto fusible web, fuse it to the wrong side of the pieced unit from step 3, and cut it out. Fuse the eagle to the tan background rectangle and stitch around the edges, using your preferred method. (I used brown thread and a decorative machine stitch.)

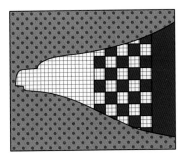

5. Using the pattern as a guide for placement, stitch the eye with pearl cotton, using an outline stitch for the lines and a satin stitch for the eye itself, as shown below and on page 71. Or draw and fill it in with a fine-point permanent marker.

6. Sew the 3" x 9¼" red strips to the sides of the Eagle block. Press the seams toward the red strips. Sew the 3" x 16¼" red strips to the top and bottom of the Eagle block. Press the seams toward the red strips.

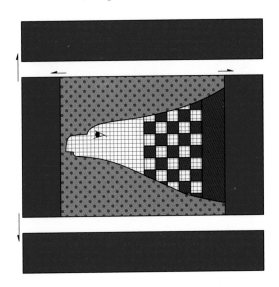

7. To create the pieced background unit, sew 10 assorted 1½" x 42" brown strips together, offsetting each strip by ½" at the edges, as shown. Repeat to make 4 sets of 10 strips each, positioning the brown strips identically in each set.

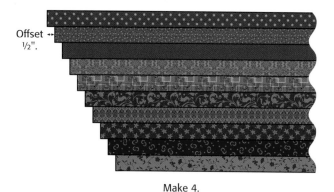

Offset ½".

Make 4.

8. Sew the four sets of brown strips together, again offsetting the edges by ½".

9. Align the 60-degree-angle line on your ruler with the seams to trim the offset edges on the sides of the piece so that the piece is 29¾" wide.

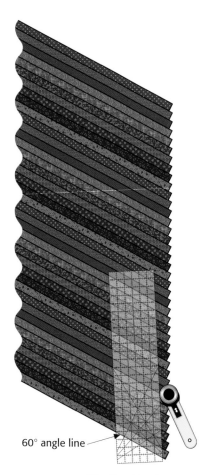

60° angle line

Trim the side edges.

10. Align the 30-degree-angle line on the ruler with the seams to trim the top and bottom edges so that the piece is 28" high.

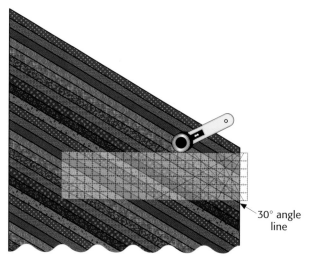

30° angle line

Trim the top and bottom edges.

11. Your rectangle should now measure 29¾" x 28". If yours is slightly larger or smaller, that's OK but be sure to adjust the length of your border pieces accordingly. (See "Borders" on page 72.) Handle the piece carefully to prevent stretching the bias edges.

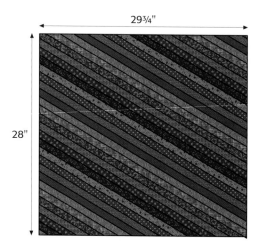

29¾"

28"

12. Sew the 2¾" x 28" black-and-tan plaid border strips to the sides of the pieced background unit. Press the seams toward the border. Sew a 2¾" brown square to each end of the 2¾" x 29¾" black-and-tan plaid border strips. Press the seams toward the border strips. Add the border strips with corner squares to the top and bottom of the pieced background unit. Press the seams toward the border.

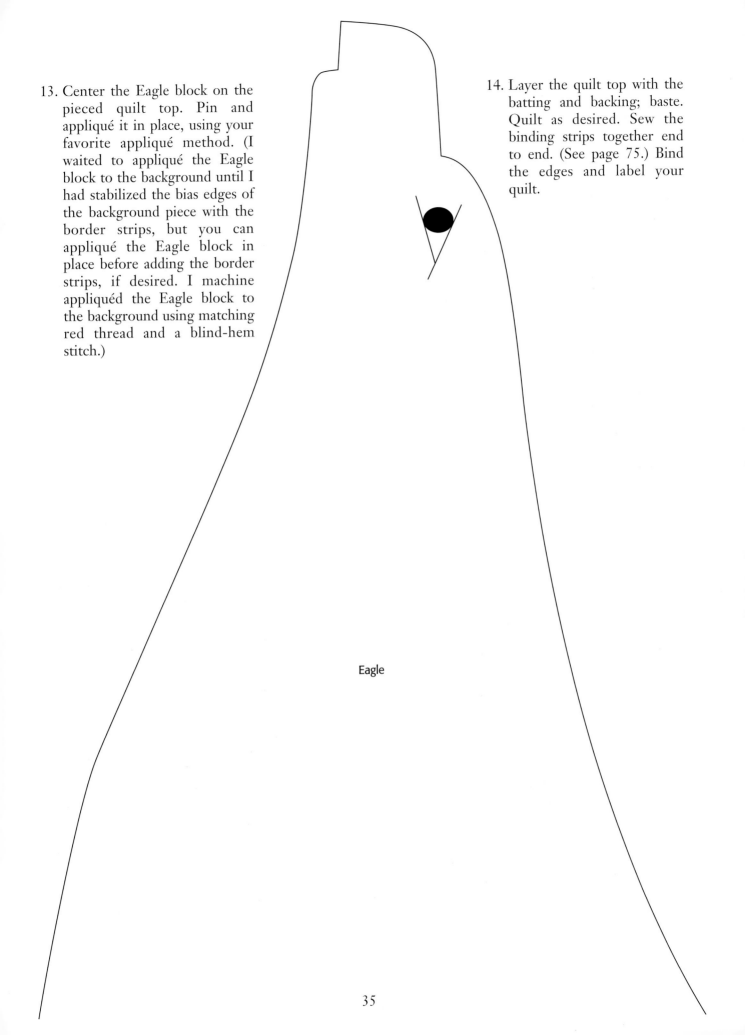

13. Center the Eagle block on the pieced quilt top. Pin and appliqué it in place, using your favorite appliqué method. (I waited to appliqué the Eagle block to the background until I had stabilized the bias edges of the background piece with the border strips, but you can appliqué the Eagle block in place before adding the border strips, if desired. I machine appliquéd the Eagle block to the background using matching red thread and a blind-hem stitch.)

14. Layer the quilt top with the batting and backing; baste. Quilt as desired. Sew the binding strips together end to end. (See page 75.) Bind the edges and label your quilt.

Eagle

Stars, Stripes, and Other Stuff

51½" x 51½". Quilted by Becky Kraus.

Simple, traditional blocks are always my favorites, and I enjoy trying to display them in unusual ways. I also like it if I don't have to match seams when I sew blocks together. In this quilt, I was able to make both Nine Patch and Rail Fence blocks, and then combine them with a simple star and a plain square—and no matching seams! Then I played with the arrangement of these four blocks, so the quilt looks more complicated than it is.

FABRIC	CUTTING
Yardage is based on 42"-wide fabric.	*Measurements include ¼" seam allowances.*
Rail Fence Blocks	
¼ yd. tan print	2 strips, 2⅛" x 42"
¼ yd. white print**	2 strips, 2⅛" x 42"
¼ yd. red print	2 strips, 2⅛" x 42"
¼ yd. dark blue print	1 strip, 2⅛" x 42" 1 strip, 1½" x 42"
⅛ yd. grayed blue print	1 strip, 2⅛" x 42"
⅛ yd. medium blue print	1 strip, 1½" x 42"
Nine Patch Blocks	
⅝ yd. red print	5 strips, 3" x 42"
½ yd. white print**	4 strips, 3" x 42"
Star Blocks	
⅔ yd. medium blue print	9 squares, 8" x 8"*
½ yd. white print**	Star pattern (page 40), 9 stars
Plain Squares	
⅓ yd. *each* of 2 blue prints	5 squares, 8" x 8", from 1 blue* 4 squares, 8" x 8", from the other blue*
¾ yd. red print for border	6 strips, 3½" x 42"
3¼ yds. for backing	
½ yd. red plaid for binding	6 strips, 2" x 42"
56" x 56" piece of batting	
½ yd. lightweight fusible web (optional)	
White pearl cotton, size 5 (optional)	
Chenille needle, size 22 (optional)	

*Note: An 8" Bias Square ruler makes cutting 8" squares easy, quick, and accurate!

**I used the same white print in the Rail Fence, Nine Patch, and Star blocks. If you wish to do the same, add the yardage amounts for these fabrics together. That means you would use 1¼ yards of just one white print.

Directions

1. There are 2 slightly different fabric arrangements for the Rail Fence blocks in this quilt. Sew together a 2⅛" strip of dark blue, a 2⅛" strip of tan, a 1½" strip of medium blue, a 2⅛" strip of white, and a 2⅛" strip of red, in that order, to make Strip Set 1. Press seams as desired. From Strip Set 1, cut five segments, each 8" wide, to make five Rail Fence blocks.

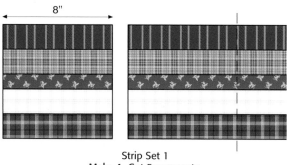

Strip Set 1
Make 1. Cut 5 segments.

2. Sew together a 2⅛" strip of tan, a 2⅛" strip of white, a 1½" strip of dark blue, a 2⅛" strip of grayed blue, and a 2⅛" strip of red, in that order, to make Strip Set 2. Press the seams as desired. From Strip Set 2, cut four segments, each 8" wide, to make four Rail Fence blocks.

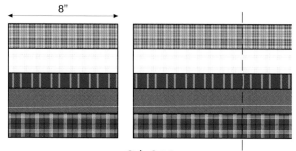

Strip Set 2
Make 1. Cut 4 segments.

3. For the Nine Patch blocks, sew a 3" x 42" red strip to each side of a 3" x 42" white strip. Press the seams toward the red strips to make Strip Set 3. Repeat to make a second Strip Set 3. From the strip sets, cut 14 segments, each 3" wide. Sew a 3" x 42" white strip to each side of

a 3" x 42" red strip to make Strip Set 4. Press the seams toward the red strip. From Strip Set 4, cut 13 segments, each 3" wide.

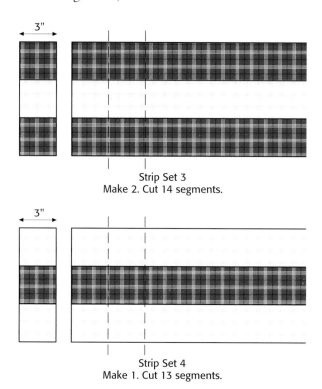

Strip Set 3
Make 2. Cut 14 segments.

Strip Set 4
Make 1. Cut 13 segments.

4. Arrange and sew together three segments to make each Nine Patch block, as shown.

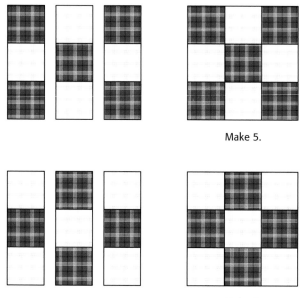

Make 5.

Make 4.

5. Referring to "Fusible Appliqué" on page 70 and using the star pattern (page 40), trace nine stars onto fusible web, fuse the web to the wrong side of a piece of white fabric, and cut out the stars. Fuse each star to an 8" x 8" medium blue square, and sew a blanket stitch around the outer edges of the stars by hand or machine. (I used white pearl cotton and made the blanket stitch by hand. See "Blanket Stitch" on page 71.)

Make 9.

6. The blocks for this quilt are arranged in 4-block sections, then stitched together in horizontal rows. Each 4-block section is a different arrangement of 1 Rail Fence block, 1 Nine Patch block, 1 Star block, and 1 plain square. See the photo on page 36 for placement, or arrange as desired. Sew the blocks together in horizontal rows, alternating pressing from row to row. Stitch the rows together.

7. Sew together three 3½" x 42" red print border strips. From the pieced strip, cut two strips, each 45½" long. Sew the strips to the sides of the quilt top. Press the seams toward the border.

8. Sew together the three remaining 3½" x 42" red print border strips. From the pieced strip, cut two strips, each 51½" long. Sew the strips to the top and bottom of the quilt top. Press the seams toward the border.

9. Piece the backing with either a horizontal or vertical seam. You will have extra fabric. Layer the quilt with the batting and backing; baste. Quilt as desired. Sew the binding strips together end to end. (See page 75.) Bind the edges and label your quilt.

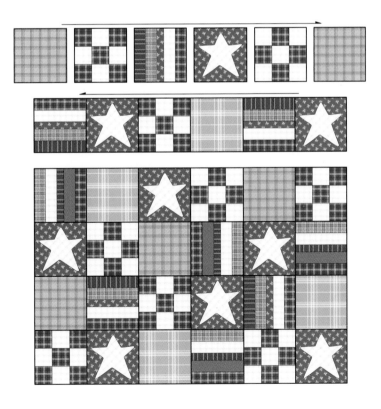

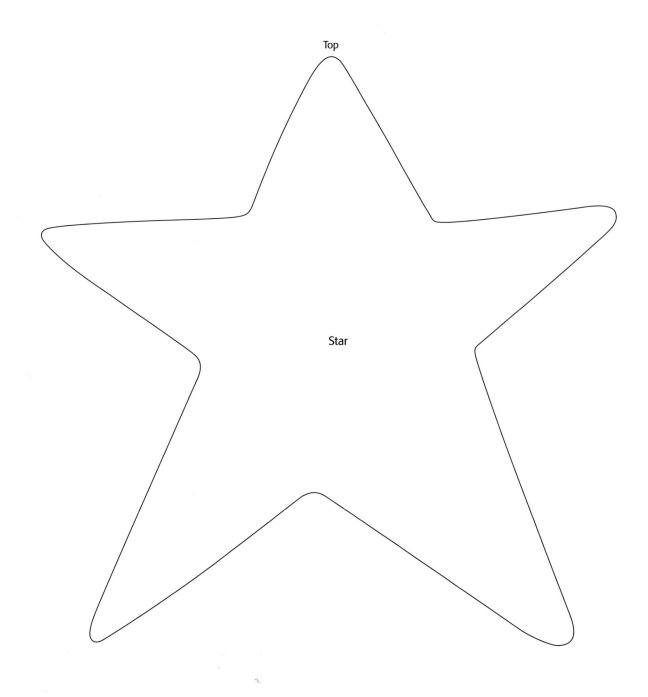

Top

Star

Lopsided Flags

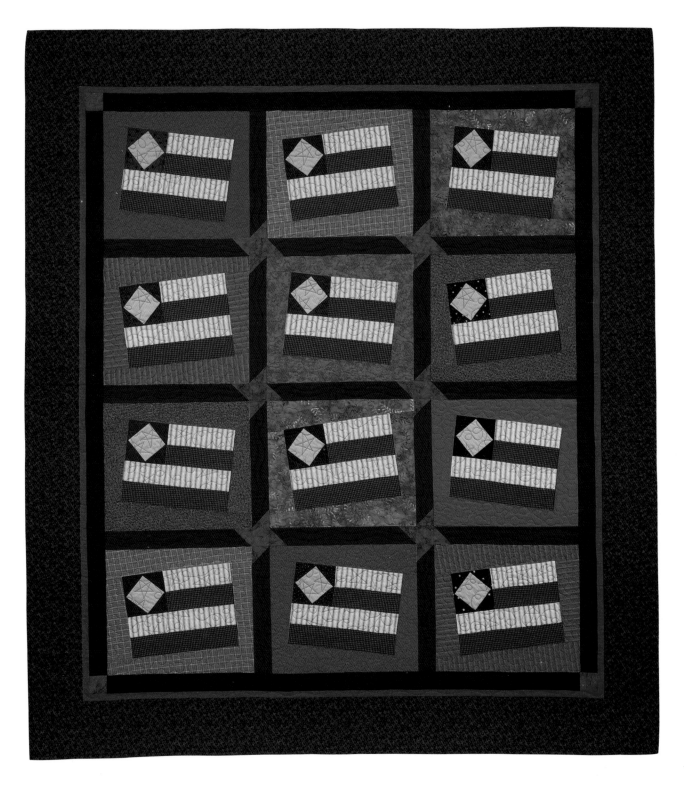

71½" x 80". Quilted by Becky Kraus.

In this quilt, I combined my love for flag blocks with the lopsided technique I've used in the past. Including flags lopsided both to the right and to the left gives this quilt a whimsical feeling.

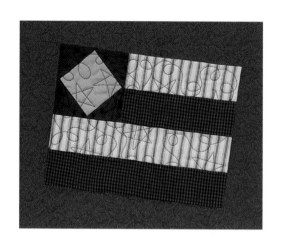

FABRIC	CUTTING
Yardage is based on 42"-wide fabric.	*Measurements include ¼" seam allowances.*
Flag Blocks	
⅔ yd. light print for stripes	7 strips, 2¾" x 42"
⅔ yd. red print for stripes	7 strips, 2¾" x 42"
⅜ yd. *total* scraps of navy blue fabrics for star units	24 squares, 3½" x 3½"; ◻ to yield 48 triangles
⅜ yd. *each* of 12 medium blue fabrics for block backgrounds	From *each* blue: 2 rectangles, 4½" x 9½" 2 rectangles, 4½" x 20½"
¼ yd. tan for star units	12 squares, 3½" x 3½"
1⅜ yds. dark blue fabric for sashing and inner border	8 rectangles, 2½" x 14½" 9 rectangles, 2½" x 17" 7 strips, 2½" x 42"
⅜ yd. red fabric for middle border	8 strips, 1¼" x 42"
⅜ yd. red print for sashing stars and corner squares	34 squares, 2½" x 2½"
2⅛ yds. dark blue print for outer border and binding	8 strips, 6½" x 42" 8 strips, 2" x 42"
4½ yds. for backing	
76" x 84" piece of batting	

DIRECTIONS

1. Mark the midpoint of the long edge of each navy blue triangle with a pin. Mark the midpoint of each side of the 3½" tan squares. Sew two matching blue triangles to opposite sides of a tan square, matching midpoints, and trim as shown. Sew two more matching blue triangles to the remaining sides of the tan square, again matching midpoints. Trim to 5" x 5" to make a star unit. Make 12 total.

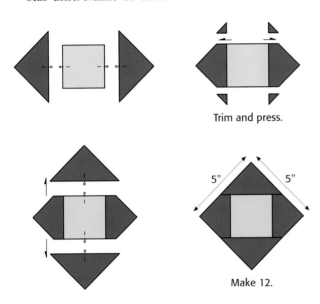

Trim and press.

Make 12.

2. To make the stripes, sew a 2¾" x 42" light strip to a 2¾" x 42" red strip to make a strip set. Press the seams toward the red strip. Repeat to make seven strip sets. From the strip sets, cut a total of twelve 8" segments and twelve 12½" segments.

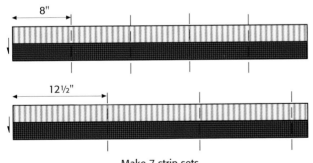

Make 7 strip sets.
From 3 strip sets, cut a total of twelve 8" segments.
From 4 strip sets, cut a total of twelve 12½" segments.

3. To make the Flag block, sew a star unit to an 8" stripe segment. Sew this unit to a 12½" stripe segment, as shown. Make 12 total.

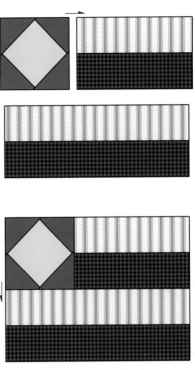

Make 12.

4. Using rectangles of the same blue fabric, sew a 4½" x 9½" medium blue rectangle to the sides of each Flag block. Press the seams toward the blue rectangles. Sew a 4½" x 20½" rectangle to the top and bottom of each Flag block. Press the seams toward the blue rectangles.

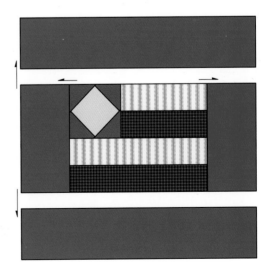

43

5. Trim the blocks as shown to get lopsided blocks. Using a ruler, trim one edge of a block at an angle as shown. After the first cut, continue around the block counterclockwise at 90-degree angles until all four sides are cut. Cut six of the blocks lopsided to the left and six lopsided to the right.

For Blocks That Slant Right

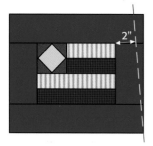

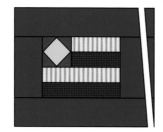

Cut #1

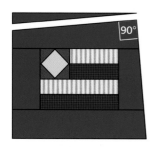

Cut #2

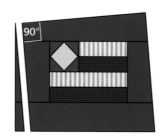

Cut #3

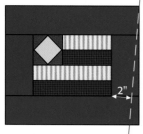

Cut #4

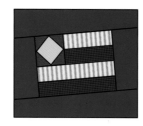

Make 6 right-slanting blocks.

For Blocks That Slant Left

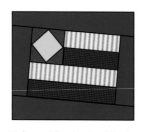

Make cut #1 at an angle as shown. Continue around block at 90° angles for cuts #2, #3, and #4.

Make 6 left-slanting blocks.

6. Trim all blocks to 14½" x 17".

7. Draw a line from corner to corner on the wrong side of twenty-four 2½" red squares. Position a 2½" red square at 1 end of a 2½" x 14½" blue sashing rectangle, placing the marked diagonal line as shown. Stitch on the diagonal line. Fold the top triangle down so the right side of the fabric is visible, and press. On the side that now has three layers of fabric, trim the seam allowance to ¼" on the bottom 2 layers, removing the triangles under the stitched unit. Repeat to make four units.

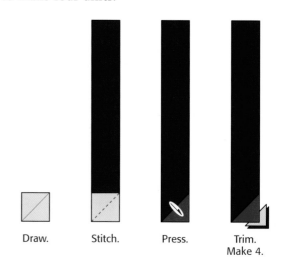

Draw.   Stitch.   Press.   Trim.
Make 4.

8. Sew a 2½" red square to each end of the remaining four 2½" x 14½" blue sashing rectangles, placing the marked diagonal lines as shown.

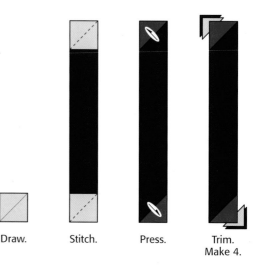

Draw.   Stitch.   Press.   Trim.
Make 4.

9. Following the method used in steps 7 and 8, sew a 2½" red square to 1 end of six 2½" x 17" blue sashing rectangles. Sew 2½" red squares to both ends of the remaining three 2½" x 17" sashing rectangles.

44

10. Join three blocks and two 14½" sashing strips to make each of the four rows, as shown.

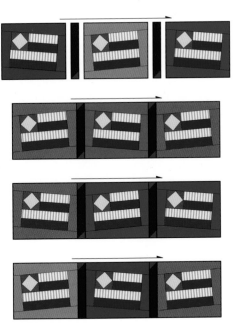

11. Join three 2½" x 17" sashing strips and two red squares to make a sashing row, as shown. Make three sashing rows.

Make 3.

12. Join the rows of blocks and sashing.

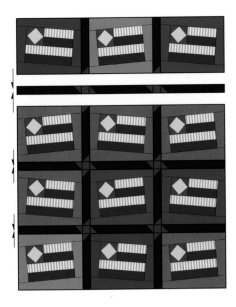

13. Sew two 2½" x 42" dark blue inner border strips together end to end. Repeat. From each pieced strip, cut a strip 62½" long. Sew 1 strip to each side of the quilt top.

14. Sew the three remaining 2½" x 42" dark blue inner border strips together end to end. From the pieced strip, cut two strips, each 54" long. Sew a 2½" red square to each end of the 2 strips. Press the seams toward the border strips. Sew the border strips with corner squares to the top and bottom of the quilt top.

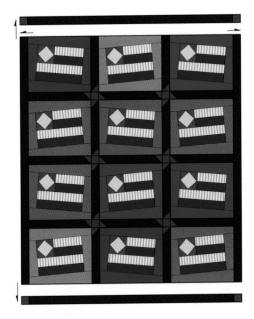

15. For the middle border, sew two 1¼" x 42" red strips together end to end. Repeat. From each pieced strip, cut a strip 66½" long. Sew the border strips to the sides of the quilt top. Press as desired.

16. Sew two more 1¼" x 42" red strips together end to end. Repeat. From each pieced strip, cut a strip 59½" long. Sew the border strips to the top and bottom of the quilt top. Press seams as desired.

17. For the outer border, sew two 6½" x 42" dark blue strips together end to end. Repeat. From each pieced strip, cut a strip 68" long. Sew the outer border strips to the sides of the quilt top. Press the seams toward the outer border.

18. Sew two more 6½" x 42" dark blue strips together end to end. Repeat. From each pieced strip, cut a strip 71½" long. Sew the outer border strips to the top and bottom of the quilt top. Press the seams toward the outer border.

19. Layer the quilt top with the batting and backing; baste. Quilt as desired. Sew the binding strips together end to end. (See page 75.) Bind the edges and label your quilt.

Patriotic Folk Animals

54½" x 61". Quilted by Becky Kraus.

I have many animals, and I love them all,
so I never tire of playing with animal
blocks. These animals, with flag bodies,
look like they're having fun—dancing,
playing, and marching across the
top of a large, pieced flag.

FABRIC	CUTTING
Yardage is based on 42"-wide fabric.	*Measurements include ¼" seam allowances.*
Animals	
⅛ yd. *each* of 4 red fabrics for flag bodies, chicken's comb and tail, dog's head, and horse's neck and head	3 rectangles, 2" x 3½"
	3 rectangles, 2" x 6½"
	4 squares, 2" x 2" (chicken's comb and tail)
	1 rectangle, 3½" x 6½" (dog's head)
	1 rectangle, 2" x 3½" (horse's neck)
	1 rectangle, 3" x 4½" (horse's head)
½ yd. taupe print for animals' legs	6 strips, cut on the bias, 1⅜" x 22"
⅛ yd. tan or beige print for flag bodies	3 rectangles, 2" x 3½"
	3 rectangles, 2" x 6½"
⅛ yd. blue solid for flag bodies	3 squares, 3½" x 3½"
⅛ yd. total scraps of blue fabrics for chicken's beak, dog's ear, and horse's ear	1 square, 2" x 2" (chicken's beak)
	Dog Ear pattern (page 52), 2 pieces
	1 square, 3½" x 3½" (horse's ear)
Flag	
¼ yd. each of 3 red prints	2 rectangles, 5" x 23"
	1 rectangle, 5" x 36½"
⅜ yd. dark blue for Star block	4 squares, 2¾" x 2¾"
	4 rectangles, 2¾" x 5"
	2 squares, 10" x 10"; ◻ to yield 4 triangles
⅜ yd. total assorted scraps of tan, beige, and/or taupe prints for Four Patch and Rail Fence blocks, half-square triangle units, and plain squares	6 rectangles, 2" x 5" (Cut 2 rectangles each from a light, a medium, and a dark print for Rail Fence blocks)
	8 squares, 2¾" x 2¾" (Four Patch blocks)
	2 squares, 5½" x 5½" (half-square triangles)
	7 squares, 5" x 5" (plain squares)

¼ yd. cream for Star block**	8 squares, 2¾" x 2¾"
	1 square, 5" x 5"
1¾ yds. cream for background of animal panel and inner border**	2 rectangles, 2" x 5" (chicken)
	1 rectangle, 2" x 3½" (chicken)
	7 squares, 2" x 2" (chicken and dog)
	1 rectangle, 3" x 3½" (horse)
	1 square, 3½" x 3½" (dog)
	1 rectangle, 3½" x 6½" (dog)
	1 rectangle, 5" x 6" (horse)
	1 square, 1½" x 1½" (horse)
	1 rectangle, 3" x 6½" (horse)
	1 rectangle, 3" x 36½" (#1)
	3 rectangles, 3" x 12" (#2, #4, #7)
	1 rectangle, 4½" x 9½" (#3)
	1 rectangle, 2½" x 12" (#5)
	1 rectangle, 3" x 9½" (#6)
	1 rectangle, 6½" x 36½" (#8)
	2 strips, 2" x 43"*
	2 strips, 2" x 39½"*
1½ yds. blue print for outer border	2 strips, 8" x 46"*
	2 strips, 8" x 39½"*
⅜ yd. red print for corner blocks	4 squares, 8" x 8"
3½ yds. for backing	
½ yd. blue fabric for binding	6 strips, 2" x 42"
59" x 65" piece of batting	
Gold or tan pearl cotton, size 5, and a chenille needle, size 22, for Xs on the animal bodies	
Dark blue pearl cotton, size 5, and a chenille needle, size 22, for the mane and tail of the horse and the tail of the dog	
4 buttons (3 small for the animals' eyes, 1 larger for the dog's nose)	

Cut on the lengthwise grain of the fabric.

**I used the same cream fabric for the background, inner border, and star. If you wish to do the same, you'll need 2 yards of cream fabric.*

ANIMAL PANEL

1. Sew a 2" x 3½" tan or beige rectangle to a 2" x 3½" red rectangle. Sew this unit to a 3½" blue square. Sew a 2" x 6½" tan or beige rectangle to a 2" x 6½" red rectangle. Sew this unit to the previous one. Stitch four Xs as shown, using gold or tan pearl cotton. Repeat to make a total of three flags for animal bodies.

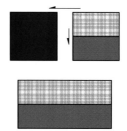
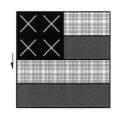

Make 3.

2. Assemble the Animal blocks by following the piecing diagrams (right). Sizes indicated are cut sizes. Block sizes will vary. To make half-square triangle units, such as the chicken's comb, beak, and tail, draw a diagonal line on the wrong side of 1 square. Layer it with the other square that makes up the triangle unit, right sides together. Stitch on the diagonal line. Fold the top triangle over so that the right side of the fabric is visible, and press. On the side that now has three layers of fabric, trim the seam allowance to ¼" on the bottom two layers, removing the triangles under the stitched unit. Each pair of squares yields 1 half-square triangle unit.

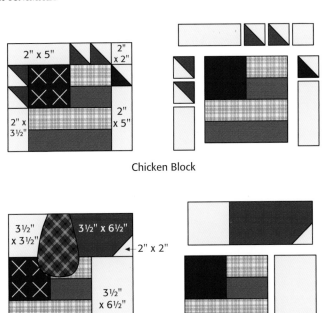

Chicken Block

Dog Block

Horse Block

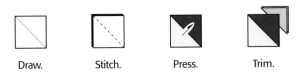

Draw. Stitch. Press. Trim.

To add triangle corners to form the jowls of the dog and horse, draw a diagonal line on the wrong side of the small square. Place it wrong side up on the appropriate corner of the larger piece. Sew on the diagonal line, trim the seam allowance to ¼", and press the triangle toward the corner. Use the Dog Ear pattern (page 52) for the dog's 3-dimensional ear, adding a ¼" seam allowance before cutting. Sew the two pieces right sides together and then turn the piece right side out. Insert the ear before stitching the seam.

Sew. Turn.

To make the horse's ear, fold the 3½" blue square as shown. Cut the folded piece in half and discard one half. Insert the remaining half (the ear) before stitching the seam.

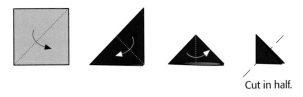

Cut in half.

3. Sew background piece #3 to the top of the chicken block. Sew piece #6 to the top of the dog block. Sew piece #2 to the left of the chicken unit, piece #4 between the chicken and the horse, piece #5 between the horse and the dog, and piece #7 to the right of the dog. (See the illustration on page 50.) Press all the seams toward the background pieces. Sew piece #1 to the top of the animal unit. Press the seam toward piece #1.

4. To make the animals' legs, fold the bias strips with wrong sides together and then stitch a ⅛" seam. Press the seam allowance to one side. When you turn the piece over, the seam should not be visible from the front. Position background piece #8 below the pieced animal unit. Glue the legs as shown or as desired, trimming excess and turning under raw edges that won't

49

be stitched into the seam. Stitch close to the edges of the legs with a straight machine stitch. (A portion of one of the horse's legs overlaps the animal unit beyond the upper edge of piece #8. Leave this portion of the leg unstitched until piece #8 is attached to the animal unit.) Sew piece #8 with the attached animal legs to the bottom of the pieced animal unit. Press the seams toward piece #8. Finish sewing the horse's leg in place.

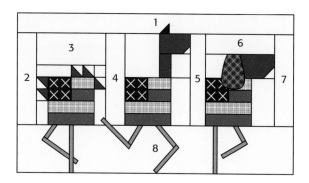

5. With blue pearl cotton and a chenille needle, referring to the the detail photos below, stitch the mane and tail on the horse and the tail on the dog using an outline stitch as shown on page 71.

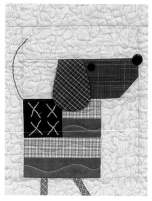

FLAG PANEL

1. To make the Four Patch blocks, sew four 2¾" squares together as shown, alternating lights and darks. Press the seams toward the darker fabric. Repeat to make 2 Four Patch blocks.

Make 2.

2. To make the half-square triangles, draw a diagonal line on the wrong side of the lighter 5½" tan, beige, or taupe square. Sew ¼" from the marked line on both sides. Cut on the marked diagonal line. Press the seams toward the darker fabric. Trim to 5" x 5".

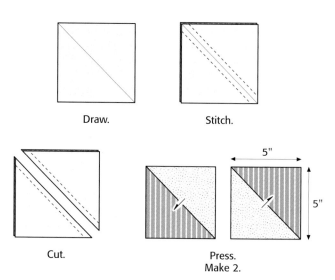

Draw. Stitch.

Cut. Press.
Make 2.

3. To make the Rail Fence blocks, arrange three rectangles in order from light to dark. Sew the rectangles together and press toward the darker fabrics.

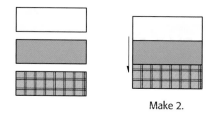

Make 2.

4. Sew the half-square triangle units, Four Patch and Rail Fence blocks, and plain squares into 2 rows, as shown. Press the seams toward the plain squares.

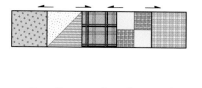
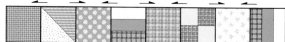

5. Sew a 5" x 23" red strip to each side of the shorter pieced block section. Sew a 5" x 36½" red strip to the bottom of the longer pieced block section. Press the seams toward the red strips.

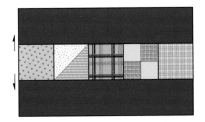

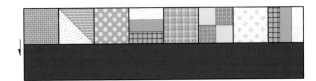

6. To make the star, I use the sew and flip method of making triangles for the star points. Draw a diagonal line on the wrong side of eight 2¾" cream squares. Position one square on one side of a 2¾" x 5" dark blue rectangle. Align three edges and sew on the diagonal line. Trim the seam allowance to ¼" and remove the corner triangles. Press the triangle to the corner of the rectangle. Sew another 2¾" cream square to the other side of the rectangle in the same manner. Repeat to make a total of four star point units.

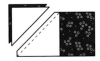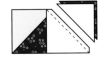

Make 4.

7. Sew two 2¾" dark blue squares to opposite sides of 2 of the star point units. Sew the remaining 2 star point units to opposite sides of the 5" cream square as shown. Press the seams toward the cream square. Sew the units together in rows to complete the star.

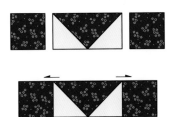

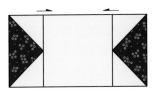

Make 2.

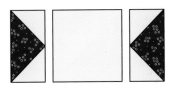

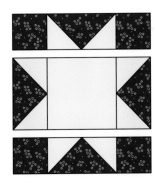

Make 1.

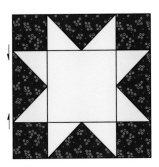

Make 1.

8. Sew two 10" dark blue triangles to opposite sides of the star. Press the seams toward the triangles. Sew two more triangles to the remaining sides of the star. Trim to 14" x 14".

Make 1.

9. Sew the Star block to the unit of two red strips and pieced blocks. Press the seams away from the Star block. Sew this to the top of the unit of one red strip and pieced blocks to complete the flag.

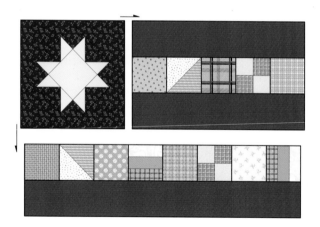

QUILT ASSEMBLY AND FINISHING

1. Sew the flag panel to the lower edge of the animal panel.

2. Sew the 2" x 43" border strips to opposite sides of the quilt top. Press the seams toward the border. Sew the 2" x 39½" border strips to the top and bottom edges of the quilt top. Press the seams toward the border.

3. Sew the 8" x 46" blue outer border strips to the sides of the quilt top. Press the seams toward the border. Sew the 8" corner blocks to the ends of the 8" x 39½" border strips. Press the seams toward the border strips, then sew these strips to the top and bottom edges of the quilt top. Press the seams toward the border.

4. Layer the quilt top with the batting and backing; baste. Quilt as desired. Referring to the photo on page 46, sew buttons on for the animals' eyes and dog's nose. Sew the binding strips together end to end. (See page 75.) Bind the edges and label your quilt.

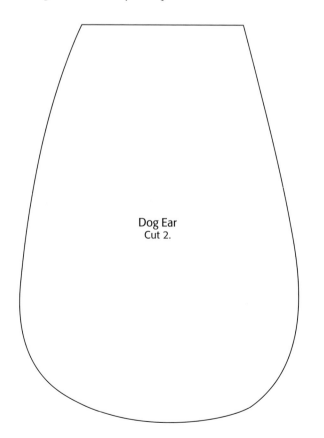

Dog Ear
Cut 2.

Starry, Starry Night

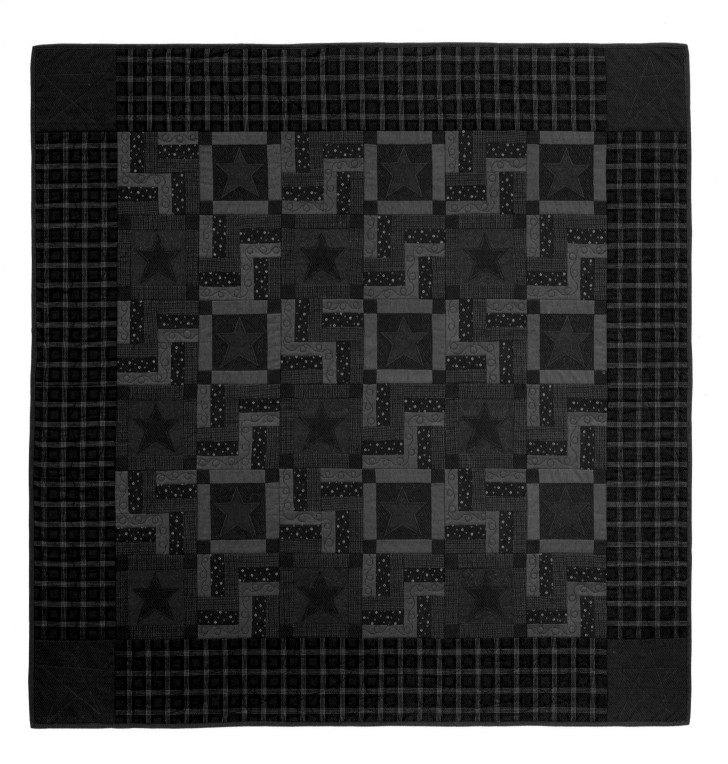

60½" x 60½". Quilted by Kathy Staley.

I enjoy challenging myself to make a quilt with enough contrast when my lightest fabric isn't very light at all! This quilt has a unique look with just medium and dark blues and reds.

FABRIC	CUTTING
Yardage is based on 42"-wide fabric.	*Measurements include ¼" seam allowances.*
Rail Fence Blocks	
⅝ yd. medium blue solid*	8 strips, 1¾" x 42"
⅝ yd. medium dark blue print #1	8 strips, 1¾" x 42"
⅝ yd. medium dark blue print #2*	8 strips, 1¾" x 42"
Star Blocks	
⅝ yd. red solid for red stars and background of blue Star blocks	Star pattern (page 56), 9 stars 9 squares, 5½" x 5½"
⅝ yd. dark blue solid for blue stars and background of red Star blocks*	Star pattern (page 56), 9 stars 9 squares, 5½" x 5½"
½ yd. medium dark blue print #2*	3 strips, 1¾" x 42"; subcut into 18 rectangles, 1¾" x 5½" 1 strip, 5½" x 42"
½ yd. medium blue solid*	3 strips, 1¾" x 42"; subcut into 18 rectangles, 1¾" x 5½" 1 strip, 5½" x 42"
⅜ yd. dark blue solid*	4 strips, 1¾" x 42"
1½ yds. red-and-blue plaid for border	4 strips, 8" x 45½"**
⅜ yd. dark blue solid for corner squares*	4 squares, 8" x 8"
2 yds. for backing	
65" x 65" piece of batting	
½ yd. red solid for binding	7 strips, 2" x 42"
1 yd. paper-backed fusible web (optional)	
Red thread to match red fabric	
Dark blue thread to match dark blue fabric	

I used the same medium blue solid in both the Rail Fence blocks and red Star blocks, the same medium dark blue print (#2) in the Rail Fence blocks and blue Star blocks, and the same dark blue solid for the blue stars, the dark blue squares in all the Star blocks, and the large corner squares in the border of the quilt. If you wish to do the same, add the yardage amounts for these colors together. That means you would use 1⅛ yds. of a medium blue solid, 1⅛ yds. of a medium dark blue print (#2), and 1⅜ yds. of a dark blue solid.
**Cut on the lengthwise grain of the fabric.*

Directions

1. Join a 1¾" x 42" medium blue, medium dark blue #1, and medium dark blue #2 strip, as shown, to make a strip set. Repeat to make eight strip sets. From the strip sets, cut 72 segments, each 4¼" wide.

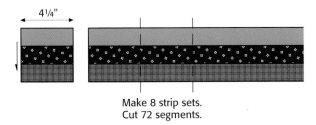

Make 8 strip sets.
Cut 72 segments.

2. Join four segments from step 1 as shown to make a Rail Fence block. Repeat to make 18 blocks.

Make 18.

3. Referring to "Fusible Appliqué" on page 70, and using the Star pattern (page 56), trace 18 stars onto fusible web. Fuse nine stars to the wrong side of the red solid and nine stars to the wrong side of the dark blue solid. Cut out the stars. Fuse the red stars to the 5½" dark blue background squares. Fuse the dark blue stars to the 5½" red background squares. Machine zigzag stitch around the edges of the stars, using thread to match the star fabric. Inside the zigzag stitch, straight stitch by machine ¼" away from the zigzag stitching, using red thread on the dark blue stars and dark blue thread on the red stars. See the photo on page 54.

4. Sew 1¾" x 42" dark blue solid strips to each side of a 5½" x 42" medium dark blue print #2 strip to make Strip Set 1. From the strip set, cut 18 segments, each 1¾" wide. In the same manner, sew 1¾" x 42" dark blue solid strips to each side of a 5½" x 42" medium blue solid strip to make

Strip Set 2. From the strip set, cut 18 segments, each 1¾" wide.

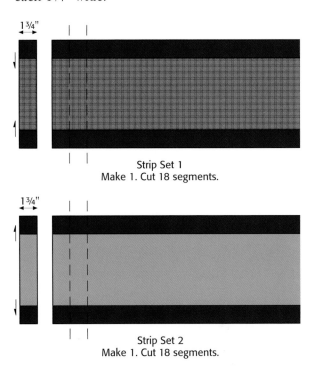

Strip Set 1
Make 1. Cut 18 segments.

Strip Set 2
Make 1. Cut 18 segments.

5. Sew a 1¾" x 5½" medium dark blue print #2 rectangle to the sides of the blue Star blocks. Complete the blue Star blocks by sewing a Strip Set 1 segment from step 4 to the top and bottom edges of the blocks. Make nine blocks total. Sew a medium blue solid 1¾" x 5½" rectangle to the sides of the red Star blocks. Complete the red Star blocks by sewing a Strip Set 2 segment from step 4 to the top and bottom edges of the blocks. Make nine blocks total.

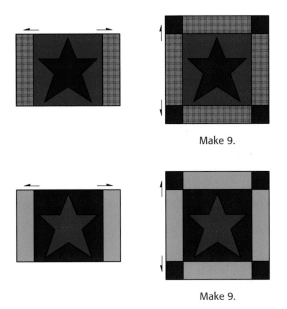

Make 9.

Make 9.

6. Arrange the blocks in six rows of six blocks each, as shown, alternating Rail Fence blocks with Star blocks. Notice that rows of red and blue stars alternate. Notice also that Rail Fence blocks are rotated in different positions. Make changes in the arrangement of blocks as desired.

7. Sew the blocks together in horizontal rows, alternating pressing from row to row. Stitch the rows together.

8. Sew two 8" x 45½" red-and-blue plaid border strips to the sides of the quilt top. Press the seams toward the border. Sew an 8" dark blue solid corner square to each end of the remaining 8" x 45½" red-and-blue plaid border strips. Press the seams toward the border strips. Sew these pieced strips to the top and bottom of the quilt top.

9. Layer the quilt top with the batting and backing; baste. Quilt as desired. Sew the binding strips together end to end. (See page 75.) Bind the edges and label your quilt.

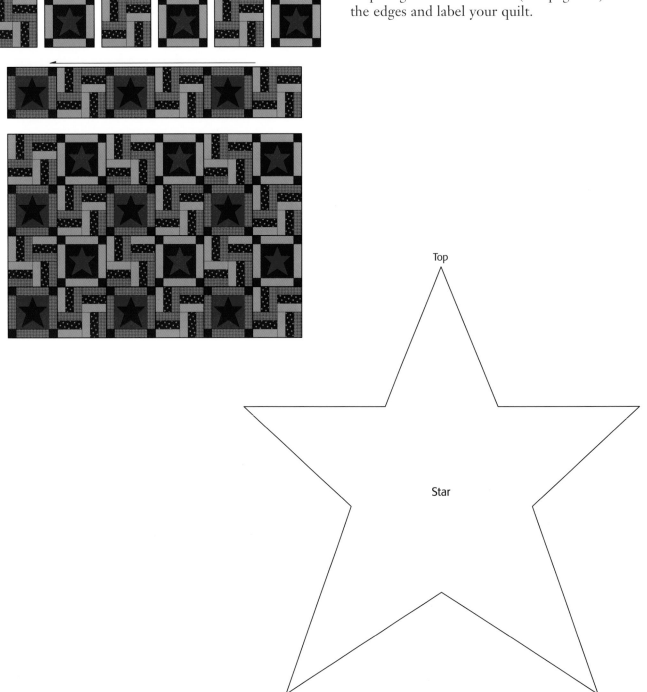

Top

Star

Old Glory

32" x 81½".
Quilted by Becky Kraus.

This was the first quilt I made for this book. I had fun playing with the different neutral tones, choosing simple pieced units and alternating them with plain squares so that no seams had to match, and picking different red fabrics (red is my favorite color). I also like the way the four Star blocks, so easy to make, look so much more elegant on point as the field of this flag.

FABRIC	CUTTING
Yardage is based on 42"-wide fabric.	*Measurements include ¼" seam allowances.*
Stripes	
⅝ yd. *total* scraps of tan, beige, and/or taupe prints for plain squares	16 squares, 5" x 5"
⅜ yd. *each* of 4 red prints*	2 strips of *each* fabric, 5" x 42"
⅛ yd. *total* of 3 tan, beige, and/or taupe prints for rail fence units	1 strip of *each* fabric, 2" x 42"
¼ yd. *total* scraps of tan, beige, and/or taupe prints for half-square triangles	6 squares, 5½" x 5½"
⅛ yd. *each* of 2 tan, beige, and/or taupe prints for four patch units	1 strip of *each* fabric, 2¾" x 42"
Stars	
½ yd. cream print for stars	4 squares, 5½" x 5½" 32 squares, 3" x 3"
1⅛ yds. blue print for background	4 strips, 3" x 42"; subcut into 16 rectangles, 3" x 5½", and 16 squares, 3" x 3" 1 strip, 1" x 42"; subcut into 2 rectangles, 1" x 10½", and 1 rectangle, 1" x 21 2 squares, 18" x 18"
2½ yds. for backing	
½ yd. red solid for binding	6 strips, 2" x 42"
36" x 86" piece of batting	

These red stripes need to be 50" long, so you will be piecing the strips together end to end. If you have a directional fabric and don't want to piece, you will need to use 1½ yds. of that fabric and cut the strips on the lengthwise grain. You'll have extra fabric, and lots of it, but it could be used for part of the quilt back.

DIRECTIONS

1. Sew the two 2¾" x 42" tan, beige, or taupe strips together to make a strip set. Press the seams toward the darker fabric. From the strip set, cut 10 segments, each 2¾" wide. Join two segments as shown to make a four patch unit. Make five units total.

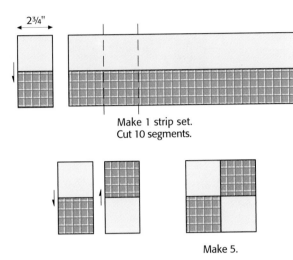

Make 1 strip set.
Cut 10 segments.

Make 5.

2. Choose two 5½" tan, beige, or taupe squares. Draw a diagonal line on the wrong side of the lighter square. Sew ¼" from the marked line on both sides. Cut on the marked diagonal line. Press the seams toward the darker fabric. Repeat with the remaining 5½" squares. Trim all half-square triangle units to 5" x 5". You will have six units total; only five are needed for this project.

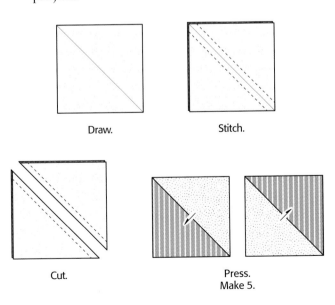

Draw.

Stitch.

Cut.

Press.
Make 5.

3. Sew the three 2" x 42" tan, beige, or taupe strips together in order from light to dark to make a strip set. Press toward the darker fabrics. From the strip set, cut seven segments, each 5" wide, to make the rail fence units.

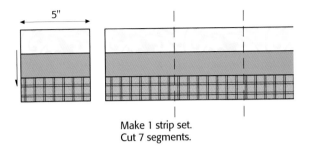

Make 1 strip set.
Cut 7 segments.

4. Arrange plain squares and the four patch, half-square triangle, and rail fence units into three strips, as shown, noting the light and dark placement in each block, or arrange blocks as desired. Sew the blocks into three strips. Press the seams toward the plain squares.

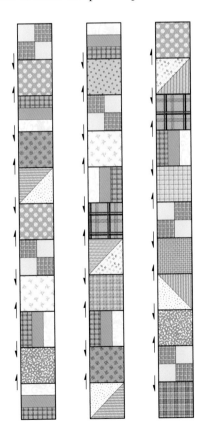

59

5. Sew two 5" x 42" red strips of the same fabric together end to end. Trim the strip to 50" long. Repeat with the remaining red strips. Sew the red strips and pieced strips together to complete the stripes section of your quilt.

6. I use the sew and flip method of making triangles for the star points. Draw a diagonal line on the wrong side of the thirty-two 3" cream squares. Position 1 square on 1 side of the 3" x 5½" blue rectangle, aligning three edges and sewing on the diagonal line. Trim the seam allowance to ¼" and remove the corner triangles. Press the triangle to the corner of the rectangle. Sew another 3" cream square to the other side of the rectangle in the same manner. Repeat to make a total of 16 star point units.

Make 16.

7. Sew two 3" blue print squares to opposite sides of one of the star point units to make Unit A. Repeat to make eight of Unit A. Sew two star point units to opposite sides of each 5½" cream square to make Unit B as shown. Press the seams toward the cream square. Repeat to make four of Unit B. Sew a Unit A to each side of a Unit B, as shown, to complete the star. Make four Star blocks total.

Unit A
Make 8.

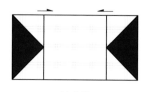

Unit B
Make 4.

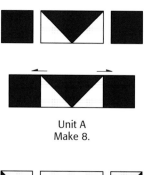

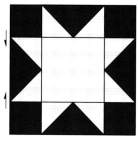

Make 4.

8. Sew two Star blocks together with a 1" x 10½" blue strip between them. Repeat.

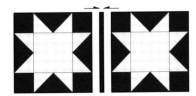

Make 2.

9. Sew the two star units together with the 1" x 21" blue strip between them.

10. Cut the two 18" blue print squares in half on the diagonal. Sew two blue triangles to opposite sides of the 4-star unit. Press the seams toward the triangles and trim as shown. Sew two more triangles to the remaining sides of the 4-star unit. Trim to 32" x 32".

11. Sew the Star block to the striped unit. Press the seams away from the Star block.

12. Layer the quilt top with the batting and backing; baste. Quilt as desired. Sew the binding strips together end to end. (See page 75.) Bind the edges and label your quilt.

Twirling Stars

62½" x 70½". Quilted by Becky Kraus.

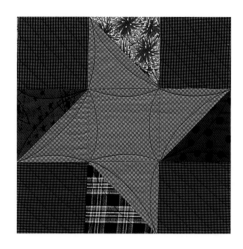

I don't usually sew triangles on the bias, but I had so much fun playing with these interlocking stars that I made an exception!

FABRIC	CUTTING
Yardage is based on 42"-wide fabric.	*Measurements include ¼" seam allowances.*
Stars	
¼ yd. *each* of 13 blue prints	2 squares of *each* blue print, 6" x 6"; ◻ to make 4 triangles
	1 square of *each* blue print, 5½" x 5½"
¼ yd. *each* of 12 gold prints	2 squares of *each* gold print, 6" x 6"; ◻ to make 4 triangles
	1 square of *each* gold print, 5½" x 5½"
3 yds. red check for background and borders	36 squares, 5½" x 5½"
	10 squares, 6" x 6"; ◻ to make 20 triangles
	3 strips, 4" x 42"
	4 strips, 8" x 42"
4 yds. for backing (horizontal seam)	
½ yd. blue fabric for binding	7 strips, 2" x 42"
6" Bias Square ruler	

DIRECTIONS

1. Arrange four blue print triangles around a matching 5½" blue print square to make a star. Repeat with the remaining blue and gold print triangles and squares, arranging the stars as desired, and using the photo on page 62 as a guide. Place the 5½" red check background squares between the stars and in the corners of the quilt top. Fill in the gaps around the outer edges of the arrangement with the red triangles.

2. Working one row at a time, pick up two adjoining triangles and sew them together along their diagonal edges. Press the seams toward the darker fabric. Trim to 5½" x 5½", using a Bias Square ruler, as shown. Place the half-square triangle unit back into the quilt arrangement. Repeat with the remaining triangle pieces.

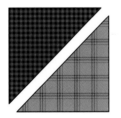 

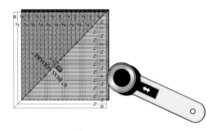

3. Sew the half-square triangle units and 5½" squares together in horizontal rows. Press the seams toward the plain squares. Sew the rows together.

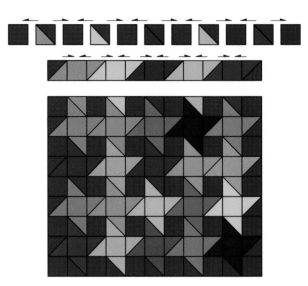

4. For the side borders, sew three 4" x 42" red print strips together end to end. Cut two strips, each 55½" long, from this strip. Sew the strips to the sides of the quilt top. Press the seams toward the border.

5. For the top and bottom borders, sew two 8" x 42" red check strips together end to end. Repeat. From each strip, cut one 62½" long strip. Sew the strips to the top and bottom of the quilt top. Press the seams toward the border.

6. Layer the quilt top with the batting and backing; baste. Quilt as desired. Sew the binding strips together end to end. (See page 75.) Bind the edges and label your quilt.

Is It Really a Flag?

59¾" x 59¾". Quilted by Becky Kraus.

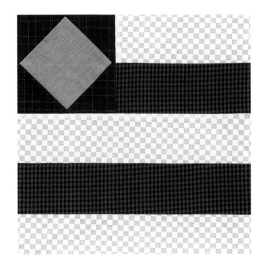

I like to play with blocks, and it's always a pleasant surprise when I can create an unexpected illusion. By repeating and rotating these Flag blocks, they don't appear to be flags at all until you study them closely!

FABRIC	CUTTING
Yardage is based on 42"-wide fabric.	*Measurements include ¼" seam allowances.*
Field (Blue and tan)	
½ yd. navy blue plaid	32 squares, 3½" x 3½"; ◲ to make 64 triangles
⅓ yd. tan print	16 squares, 3½" x 3½"
Stripes	
1¾ yds. white	20 strips, 2¾" x 42" 1 square, 2¾" x 2¾"
1 yd. red check*	10 strips, 2¾" x 42"
1¼ yds. navy blue print for borders	6 strips, 6½" x 42"
3¾ yds. for backing	
½ yd. red check for binding*	6 strips, 2" x 42"

*I used the same red fabric in the flag and for the binding. If you want to do the same, add the two yardage amounts together and use 1½ yds. of one red print.

DIRECTIONS

1. "Stars" are created with tan and navy blue squares. Sew two 3½" navy blue triangles to opposite sides of a 3½" tan square, centering the triangles. Press the seams toward the triangles. Trim as shown. Sew two more 3½" navy blue triangles to the remaining sides of the tan square, again centering the triangles. Press the seams toward the triangles. Trim the square to 5" x 5".

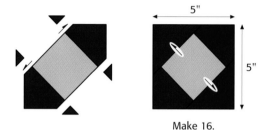

Make 16.

2. Sew a 2¾" x 42" white strip to a 2¾" x 42" red strip to make a strip set. Repeat to make a total of four strip sets. From the strip sets, cut 16 segments, each 7¼" wide.

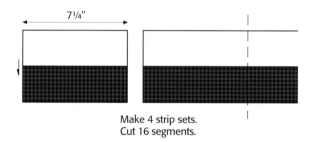

Make 4 strip sets.
Cut 16 segments.

3. Sew a 2¾" x 42" white strip to each side of a 2¾" x 42" red strip to make a strip set. Repeat to make six strip sets. From the strip sets, cut 16 segments, 11¾" wide.

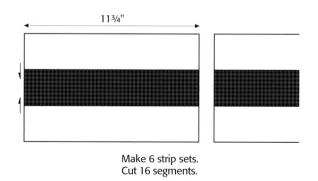

Make 6 strip sets.
Cut 16 segments.

4. Sew a "star" block to a 7¼" stripe segment. Press the seams toward the stripes. Sew this unit to an 11¾" stripe segment to complete the Flag block.

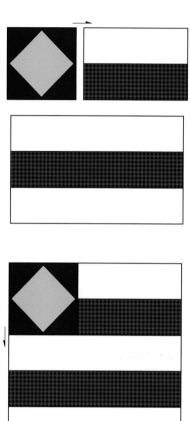

Make 16.

5. Arrange the Flag blocks into four groups of four blocks as shown, rotating each flag a quarter turn in each group of four blocks. Sew the blocks together. Press the seams as desired.

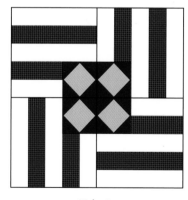

Make 4.

67

6. From the 2¾" x 42" white strips, cut four 23"-long strips. Sew a 23" white strip to one edge of each 4-block section. Press seam toward the white strip.

7. Sew the 2¾" white square to one of the 4-block units with a partial seam, as shown. Backstitch for strength in the middle of the 2¾" square.

8. Arrange this unit and the remaining three 4-block units as shown. Sew the upper left unit to the lower left unit. Press the seam toward the upper left unit. Then add the upper right unit

followed by the lower right unit, pressing seams toward the unit you just added. Complete by sewing the lower right unit to the lower left unit, completing the partial seam along the 2¾" white square.

9. Sew three 6½" x 42" navy blue strips together end to end. From the pieced strip, cut two border strips 47¾" long. Sew the strips to the sides of the quilt top. Press the seams toward the border.
10. Sew the three remaining 6½" x 42" navy blue strips together end to end. From the pieced strip, cut two border strips 59¾" long. Sew the strips to the top and bottom of the quilt top. Press the seams toward the border.
11. Layer the quilt top with the batting and backing; baste. Quilt as desired. Sew the binding strips together end to end. (See page 75.) Bind the edges and label your quilt.

Quiltmaking Basics

There are many books with extensive information on "the basics." I've tried to keep this section short and sweet, sharing with you guidelines that I've learned over the years, and information and techniques specific to the projects in this book.

What's the most fundamental thing I've learned after many years of quilting? That quilting rules are really guidelines, and that once you know them, you get to break them. Rules are not etched in stone. Someone like you and me created them. Therefore, once you know the rules and feel comfortable with them (after all, they *are* useful in guiding you, especially when you're learning), then you get to break them. Some of my most interesting and creative ideas have come from breaking the rules, daring to make mistakes (read: that's not the way it's usually done) and then fixing them.

FABRIC AND COLOR SELECTION

Use colors you like in your quilts. You have to live with your quilts, so you should like them. If you like a quilt pattern in this book but not the colors I've chosen, make the quilt in any colors you choose. Also, keep in mind that *any* quilt can be made in Americana colors.

No matter how many fabrics and colors you choose for your quilt, make sure that you create contrast. Most quilts look better when some fabrics are light in value, some are dark, and others are medium, but this is not always the case. In "Stitch It! America" on page 18, my lightest fabric is a gold—and it's really not very light at all. In order for those blocks to stand out, I made sure I used a darker fabric to contrast (the navy blue). If you don't have a full range of values, you need to be more careful in creating contrast. And always remember to judge lightness or darkness from a distance—that means 10 feet or more away. We see most of our quilts on a wall or a bed when we're standing across the room. The only time we're really up-close and personal with our fabric is when we buy it, cut it, and sew it. For the rest of its life, we see it from a distance, as part of a quilt, so that's the basis on which we need to make our choices.

Don't worry about matching colors and patterns. Quilts are much more interesting if their colors aren't perfectly matched. Our grandmothers certainly couldn't match either colors or patterns most of the time, but they still created wonderfully charming quilts. It's the mismatching that makes their quilts so interesting.

When in doubt, make a sample. I often make a sample to be sure I understand how to make the blocks or to check that I've done the math correctly. If there is something wrong with the sample block, it often becomes a label on the back of my quilt.

Use a design wall when you're ready to design your quilt. Since it's a vertical surface, everything is the same distance from your eyes. (When you lay your blocks out on the floor or another horizontal surface, some blocks are closer to you and some are farther away.) A vertical surface gives you a better perspective, and you can more easily decide if your blocks look balanced.

Allow yourself the freedom to change your mind. If the border fabric you were planning to use doesn't look good when you get your blocks put together, don't use it just because you bought it. It won't look any better after it's sewn into the quilt. Often the fabric we change our minds about can be used on the back (meaning you won't have to buy as much backing fabric), used for pillows to go with our quilt, or saved for another project. Don't force something that doesn't work.

As you work on your quilt, keep in mind that you know more than you think you know. You may not have gone to art school (most quilters haven't), but you've been looking at color, design, and balance since you were old enough to notice. You just may not have the art words for these concepts. Trust your gut feelings.

SEWING ACCURATE SEAM ALLOWANCES

All of the quilts in this book are pieced. The single most important thing to do when piecing quilts is to maintain a consistent ¼"-wide seam allowance. If you don't do this, your blocks won't be the desired finished size. When that happens, the size of everything else in the quilt is affected—alternate blocks, sashing, and borders. Measurements for all components of a quilt are based on blocks that finish at the required size.

How to Create an Accurate Seam Allowance

Some sewing machines have a ¼" presser foot, or you can purchase one. With a ¼" presser foot, you can use the edge of the foot as a guide for your fabric. The standard presser feet for most machines are wider than ¼". But you can still get an accurate ¼" seam allowance without a special foot (and very cheaply) by using masking or electrical tape to mark the distance on your machine. I like electrical tape because the colors contrast with the color of my machine, making it easy for me to see.

To get an accurate ¼" seam, place a ruler under your presser foot. Gently lower the needle onto the first ¼" line in from the right-hand edge of the ruler. Place a piece of tape along the right-hand edge of the ruler, in front of the needle, as shown.

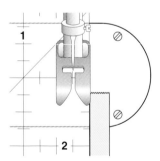

Sew a sample to test your new guide and make sure your seams are ¼" wide; if they are not, readjust your tape. Many quilters find that they need to take a scant ¼" seam rather than a full ¼" seam to get their blocks the right size.

FUSIBLE APPLIQUÉ

Some of the quilts in this book include appliquéd designs. Instructions are given here for fusible appliqué. You can substitute another appliqué method, if desired; just remember to add seam allowances to your appliqué shapes, depending on the appliqué method you use. No seam allowances are added for fusible appliqué.

Using fusible web to secure your appliqués in place is fast and fun. Refer to the manufacturer's directions when applying it; each kind is a little different.

1. Trace the appliqué pattern onto the paper side of the fusible web. Cut out the shape, leaving a generous margin all around the outline. *Note:* If the appliqué pattern is directional, you need to make a reverse tracing so the pattern will match the original when pressed in place. Otherwise, you'll get a reversed image.

2. Fuse the shape to the wrong side of your fabric.

3. Cut out the shape exactly on the line.

4. Remove the paper, position the shape on the background, and press it in place.

Although heavyweight fusibles allow you to leave appliquéd edges unsecured, even for laundering, they tend to make the shapes very stiff. I prefer to use a lightweight paper-backed fusible web such as Trans-Web or HeatnBond Lite. To prevent the exposed edges from curling, fraying, or both, I secure them with a blanket stitch (right) by hand or use a decorative machine stitch.

EMBROIDERY STITCHES

Some of the qilts in this book are embellished with embroidery stitches. Instructions are given here for the three types of stitches I used. You may substitute other stitches if desired. I used size 5 pearl cotton and a size 22 chenille needle for my stitching. I modified the running stitch shown here in "Stitch It! America" (page 18) by making the stitches long and the spaces between the stitches very short.

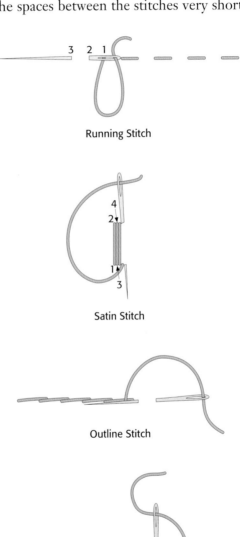

Running Stitch

Satin Stitch

Outline Stitch

Blanket Stitch

Finishing Your Quilt

In this section, I share techniques and ideas for finishing your quilt that have worked for me. Here you'll find general information about borders, batting, backing, layering and basting, quilting, binding, and labels. If you have a favorite way of doing something—for example, a special method of binding your quilt—please continue doing it your way. Different things work for different people, and in no endeavor is this truer than in quiltmaking.

Borders

Every quilt project in this book gives you information about the project's borders. If, however, you are changing the size of a quilt, you will find the following information useful.

For plain borders (without corner squares), first measure the quilt top vertically through the center. Cut two border strips to match the measurement, then sew them to the sides of the quilt top. Measure the top again horizontally through the center, including the borders you just added. Cut two border strips to match the measurement, then sew them to the top and bottom of the quilt. Press the seam allowances toward the borders.

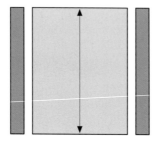

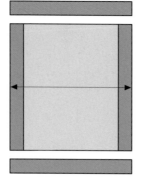

HINT

❖ Long borders are difficult to measure accurately with your 24" ruler. This is the one time that I use my cutting mat to measure fabric. Most cutting mats are at least 36" long, and some are longer. For long borders, fold the border strips in half and then trim them to the right size. That way, you should be able to use your 36" (or longer) mat for most quilts.

❖ When you add borders, fold the strips to find their midpoints and quarter points. Mark them with creases or pins. Do the same with your quilt top. Then match the midpoints, quarter points, and ends before sewing your border to your quilt top. If you do this, you won't have extra fabric to create a tuck as you approach the end of your seam.

For borders with corner squares, measure the quilt top through the center, both horizontally and vertically, and cut two border strips to match each measurement. Add border strips to the sides of the quilt top first. Sew corner squares to the remaining border strips, and add these to the top and bottom of the quilt top. Press the seam allowances toward the borders.

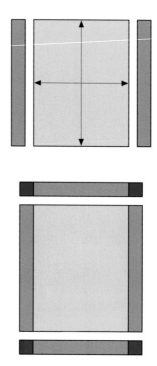

If you need to piece border strips to make them fit your quilt top, join them with a diagonal seam. Trim the seam allowances to ¼" and then press the seams open.

Batting

We have more batting choices than ever before! I am partial to cotton battings and have enjoyed the lighter weight of Quilter's Dream Cotton's Request (the thinnest batting—almost like a piece of flannel) and Select (the next thinnest), as well as my old favorite, Warm and Natural. Remember that battings can help you adjust for weight in a quilt. If you're making a large quilt but don't want it to be too heavy, consider using a thinner cotton batting. It'll make your queen-size quilt much lighter! Lighter-weight cotton battings are also easier to hand quilt.

Backing

Cut the backing at least 4" larger than your quilt top.

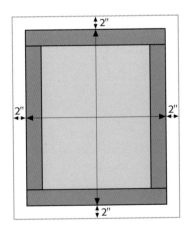

If this required measurement is wider than the width of your backing fabric, piece two lengths or widths of backing fabric together.

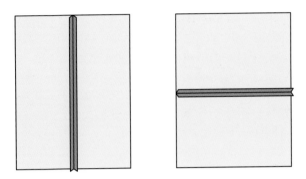

> **HINT**
> Often you will need less backing fabric if you use a horizontal rather than a vertical seam. Always figure the yardage requirements both ways, and then pin a note on your fabric so you don't forget what your plan was!

If the backing needs to be only a few inches wider than the fabric width, I often add a strip down the middle. The strip can be a single piece of fabric, or it can be pieced from leftovers—either leftover blocks from the front or leftover fabrics that you didn't use.

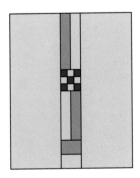

Layering and Basting

You may not even need to layer and baste your quilt if you are having it professionally machine quilted. Most machine quilters will do the layering for you, and their machines don't require basting. When in doubt, be sure to ask.

The quilt sandwich is made up of the quilt top, batting, and backing.

1. Unroll the batting, and let it relax overnight if it's polyester. (That's not necessary if it's cotton.) Cut the batting to the same size as the backing (at least 4" larger than the quilt top).
2. Place the backing, wrong side up, on a large table. Use masking tape to anchor the backing to the table. Make sure the backing is flat and wrinkle free, but be careful not to stretch it.
3. Place the batting on top of the backing, smoothing out all the wrinkles.
4. Center the pressed quilt top, right side up, on top of the batting. Again, smooth out any wrinkles. Make sure the quilt top edges are parallel to the backing edges.
5. Baste with a needle and thread if hand quilting, or with small safety pins if machine quilting.

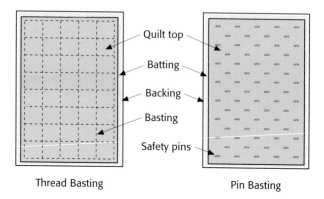

Thread Basting   Pin Basting

Quilting

There are many quilting options. You can hand or machine quilt. You can pay someone to machine quilt for you (my choice most of the time). Or you can even pay someone to hand quilt for you.

If you are doing your own quilting, start in the center and work toward the outside edges. Make sure you use a walking (or dual feed) foot on your machine when you machine quilt, unless you are dropping the feed dogs to do free-motion work.

I am often asked by my students which quilting designs would be best for their quilts. The honest answer is that there is an endless number of quilting designs that would work for any quilt. Let your blocks suggest ideas. In "What Goes Around Comes Around" (see page 26), Becky Kraus machine quilted circles that echo the circular flags.

When in doubt, stippling (a wiggly line that you make by dropping the feed dogs) is always a good choice. In "Starry, Starry Night" (see page 53), Kathy Staley's stippling helped the stars pop out and be more noticeable.

Consider matching quilting designs with the subject of the quilt. In the flag quilt "Old Glory" (see page 57), Becky Kraus quilted parallel wiggly lines in the same direction as the stripes to suggest a waving flag.

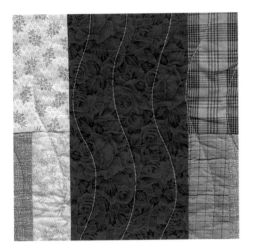

Binding

My preferred binding is a double-layer, straight-grain binding that finishes to approximately ¼". (I use a bias binding only when I want to show off a stripe or a plaid, since I need much more fabric to cut the bias strips.)

1. For straight-grain strips, cut enough 2"-wide strips across the width of the fabric to go around the perimeter of the quilt, plus 10". For bias strips, cut 2"-wide strips at a 45-degree angle to the straight of grain. Sew the strips together end to end with a diagonal seam. Trim the seam allowances to ¼", and press the seams open.

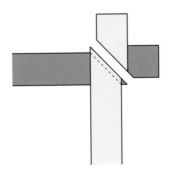

2. Cut one end of the pieced strip at a 45-degree angle. (You don't need to measure this; just eyeball it.) Fold ¼" of the angled end to the wrong side, then press. Press the entire strip in half lengthwise with wrong sides together.

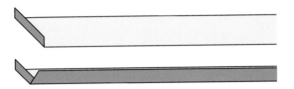

3. Start on a straight edge, not in a corner. Place the angled end of the binding along the quilt top, aligning the raw edges of the binding with the raw edges of the quilt top. Using a ¼" seam allowance, begin machine stitching about 3" from the angled end. Backstitch to secure.

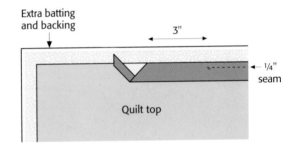

4. When you get close to a corner, insert a pin ¼" from the edge of the quilt top (eyeball it), sew up to the pin, and backstitch.

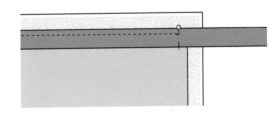

5. Remove the quilt from the machine. Fold the binding up and away from the quilt, then back down, so the fold aligns with the edge you just stitched. Align the raw edges of the binding with the next raw edge of the quilt. Begin stitching at the very edge. Don't backstitch. Repeat with the remaining corners.

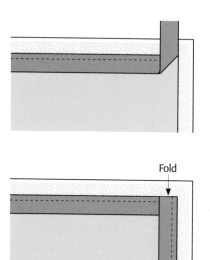

Fold

6. When you get close to where you started, insert the binding strip inside the angled end; trim if it's too long. Continue stitching a little past where you began.

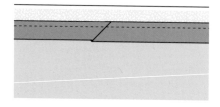

7. If you haven't done it already, trim the batting and backing even with the edges of the quilt top.

8. Finish the back by hand with a slip stitch, matching the thread color to the binding. There will be a natural miter on the front corners. Fold a miter on the back.

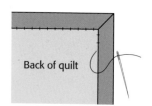

Back of quilt

Labels

The best advice I can give you about labels is to just do it: Always label your quilt. This doesn't mean you have to create a fancy label. If the backing fabric of your quilt is light, you can write label information right on the quilt back. I do this after I've bound the quilt. Then I can use the edge of the binding as my "line" to write on. If your quilt back is dark and you have an extra block you didn't use on the front, this can become a signature block. On a light part of this block, write the essential information: your name, city, state, and the year the quilt was completed. I usually write, at least, "Made by Sandy Bonsib, Issaquah, Washington, 2002." You can write much more if you want to, of course. But wouldn't you be thrilled if your grandmother had written just this much on every one of her quilts? You never know what will be cherished and passed down to the next generation. When it comes to labeling, just do it.

Bibliography

DeBarr, Candice M. and Jack A. Bonkowske. *Saga of the American Flag: An Illustrated History.* New York: Harbinger House, 1990.

Hinrichs, Kit and Delphine Hirasuna. *Long May She Wave: A Graphic History of the American Flag.* Berkeley: Ten Speed Press, 2001.

Quaife, Milo M., Melvin J. Weig, and Roy E. Appleman. *The History of the United States Flag: From the Revolution to the Present, Including a Guide to Its Use and Display.* New York: Harper and Row, 1961.

Walton, Stewart and Sally. *Folk Art: Style and Design.* New York: Sterling Publishing Co., Inc., 1993.

About the Author

Sandy Bonsib is a teacher by profession and a quilter by passion. She has a graduate degree in education. This is her fifth book. She has appeared on *Lap Quilting with Georgia Bonesteel*, *Simply Quilts* with Alex Anderson, and was one of six featured artists on *Quilts of the Northwest, 1998*. Sandy coordinates Quilts for the Children, a group that makes quilts for the children of battered women. In the past three years, this group has made over 1,000 quilts. Sandy lives on a small farm on Cougar mountain in Issaquah, Washington with her family and many animals. She also raises puppies for Guide Dogs for the Blind.

new and bestselling titles from

America's Best-Loved Craft & Hobby Books™

That Patchwork Place®

America's Best-Loved Quilt Books®

NEW RELEASES
1000 Great Quilt Blocks
American Stenciled Quilts
Americana Quilts
Appliquilt in the Cabin
Bed and Breakfast Quilts
Best of Black Mountain Quilts, The
Beyond the Blocks
Blissful Bath, The
Celebrations!
Color-Blend Appliqué
Fabulous Quilts from Favorite Patterns
Feathers That Fly
Handcrafted Garden Accents
Handprint Quilts
Knitted Throws and More for the Simply
   Beautiful Home
Knitter's Book of Finishing Techniques, The
Knitter's Template, A
Make Room for Christmas Quilts
More Paintbox Knits
Painted Whimsies
Patriotic Little Quilts
Quick Quilts Using Quick Bias
Quick-Change Quilts
Quilts for Mantels and More
Snuggle Up
Split-Diamond Dazzlers
Stack the Deck!
Strips and Strings
Sweet Dreams
Treasury of Rowan Knits, A
Triangle Tricks
Triangle-Free Quilts

APPLIQUÉ
Artful Album Quilts
Artful Appliqué
Blossoms in Winter
Easy Art of Appliqué, The
Fun with Sunbonnet Sue
Sunbonnet Sue All through the Year

BABY QUILTS
Easy Paper-Pieced Baby Quilts
Even More Quilts for Baby
More Quilts for Baby
Play Quilts
Quilted Nursery, The
Quilts for Baby

HOLIDAY QUILTS
Christmas at That Patchwork Place®
Christmas Cats and Dogs
Creepy Crafty Halloween
Handcrafted Christmas, A
Welcome to the North Pole

LEARNING TO QUILT
Joy of Quilting, The
Nickel Quilts
Quick Watercolor Quilts
Quilts from Aunt Amy
Simple Joys of Quilting, The
Your First Quilt Book (or it should be!)

PAPER PIECING
40 Bright and Bold Paper-Pieced Blocks
50 Fabulous Paper-Pieced Stars
For the Birds
Quilter's Ark, A
Rich Traditions

ROTARY CUTTING
101 Fabulous Rotary-Cut Quilts
365 Quilt Blocks a Year Perpetual Calendar
Around the Block Again
Around the Block with Judy Hopkins
Log Cabin Fever
More Fat Quarter Quilts

TOPICS IN QUILTMAKING
Batik Beauties
Frayed-Edge Fun
Log Cabin Fever
Machine Quilting Made Easy
Quick Watercolor Quilts
Reversible Quilts

CRAFTS
300 Papermaking Recipes
ABCs of Making Teddy Bears, The
Creating with Paint
Handcrafted Frames
Painted Chairs
Stamp in Color
Stamp with Style

KNITTING & CROCHET
365 Knitting Stitches a Year Perpetual
   Calendar
Clever Knits
Crochet for Babies and Toddlers
Crocheted Sweaters
Irresistible Knits
Knitted Shawls, Stoles, and Scarves
Knitted Sweaters for Every Season
Knitting with Novelty Yarns
Paintbox Knits
Simply Beautiful Sweaters
Simply Beautiful Sweaters for Men
Too Cute! Cotton Knits for Toddlers
Ultimate Knitter's Guide, The

Our books are available at bookstores and your favorite craft, fabric, and yarn retailers. If you don't see the title you're looking for, visit us at **www.martingale-pub.com** or contact us at:

1-800-426-3126

International: 1-425-483-3313

Fax: 1-425-486-7596

E-mail: info@martingale-pub.com

For more information and a full list of our titles, visit our Web site.
